I0430176

THE UNITED STATES FEDERAL GOVERNMENT, ALL THINGS TO ALL PEOPLE

OR

WHY YOUR TAXES WERE FIFTEEN PERCENT AND WHY THEY ARE GOING TO BE FIFTY PERCENT

BY

JOHN BRICKEL

Copyright applied for, 2014. All rights reserved.

Dedicated to our Congress
without whom this book would not be possible.

INTRODUCTION

For every program in your State that the United States Federal Government pays for, money from taxpayers in your State as well as forty-nine other States is required. Put another way: you and the Citizens of your State are funding programs in forty-nine other States. Do you really think you're getting your money's worth?

Without blaming Congress for everything and giving away the point of this... whups. Oh well, have you ever wondered why parties in Congress become so polarized and why they spout rhetoric seemingly about the same subject but with alarmingly different points of view? So did I and to help us suss this out I would like to introduce a term, a couple of terms really and the first one is 'Common Frame of Reference'.

For our purposes a common frame of reference is a fact over which there is no dispute. And that is important because if you listen closely to the world around you, the lack of this singular agreement is everywhere. The simplest example is almost any advertisement you see on television that uses the word 'better'. They might say their car is BETTER! or their detergent is BETTER! Well, better than what? Is it better than it was last year or is it better than its competitors? The marketer is relying on that lack of 'what' to lure you into buying their product. For instance, you may have tried that detergent a year ago and thought it was crap so when you see the word 'BETTER!' your inclination is to think that it is better than it was last year and so it is worth another try. Alternatively, you might use another brand and think that the advertised detergent is better than yours and so you should consider switching. Once again, exactly *what* do they mean by BETTER!?

That 'what' is a common frame of reference. How can we have an intelligent conversation about that car or that detergent if it is impossible to know the meaning of 'what'? All too often, Congress becomes polarized around arguments that have no common definition of that 'what' which leads us to our second phrase, 'Definition of Terms'.

One problem in politics, and you can hear it in any political debate, is the lack of an agreement due to misunderstandings - deliberate or otherwise - over what something actually means. In most industries you can find a booklet or web page with a title like Data Dictionary, Terminology or Definitions. We will use the phrase 'Definition of Terms' (DoT). These pages will be riddled with DoTs such as in the following paragraph, mostly so that we can lead by example but also because we don't want to appear hypocritical especially after a chapter like Legislative Dysfunction.

DoT: Gender. I realize parts of this are likely to be sensational but in these days of political correctness I'm going to take a chance on grammatical correctness and not worry about it. Use of the terms 'men', 'he' and 'they', are merely forms of correct grammar when gender is unknown. In this work, unless otherwise qualified, all these words pertain to members of Congress, irrespective of their gender or lack thereof.

As you can see, DoTs are how we are going to define something and how we are going to create common frames of reference. With that said, this is not some deeply esoteric argument and there is no danger of being mired in page after tedious page of fine print. It is a simple and straightforward perspective of what is going on, why taxes are going up and up and up and what we can do about it. I hope you will find it interesting, entertaining and enjoyable.

Before Federal Income Tax

Ah, the turn of the Twentieth Century, 1900 Anno Domini (or CE if you're into that), the United States of America. Oil, agriculture, industry, it was a veritable boomtown and no Federal Income Tax. Not a lick. Not until 1913 or 1909 depending on your DoT.

DoT: Amendment 16. Congress passed the 16th Amendment to the Constitution in 1909 and the States ratified it by 1913. It went into effect in 1913 meaning that our present day April 15th really started in 1914 at the rate of one to seven percent depending on your income of between zero and five hundred thousand dollars. The one percent bracket was zero to twenty thousand dollars. In 2014 dollars, that $20,000 adjusted for inflation would be a bit more than $476,000. You read that correctly.

Of course, it's not entirely true that Federal Taxation didn't start until 1913. Congress created a Federal Income Tax in 1861 to pay for the Civil War. But wait a minute - they repealed it in 1871! There's a shocker. It's exactly these sorts of things that make you wonder what happened to the timber of our elected officials. They did try a flat tax in 1894 but the Supreme Court said nope, unconstitutional. What the Hell?

Which leaves us wondering not only 'What the Hell?' but how the United States Federal Government got its money before Federal Income Tax. It's perplexing to say the least. Like the universe before the Big Bang or before we started getting screwed and not getting kissed. One percent. Really? But, I digress.

So how did the United States Federal Government get its money without a Federal Income Tax? Primarily, tariffs on various imports and a tax on whiskey. I like whiskey, not a lot, just the occasional shot will do... in fact, I'm having one now. But I digress. They must have drunk quite a bit of whiskey. And still I digress.

1913

At last, 1913, the year we got our very own, modern United States Federal Income Tax. Finally, one that wouldn't be repealed by Congress, one that wouldn't be struck down by the Supreme Court, one that we could wrap our arms around and call our very own, one that we could count on from the day we were born until April of the year following our deaths. But why did Congress want it in the first place?

Prior to this last and lasting Federal Income Tax, you could argue that the Federal Government made most of its revenue via tariffs and that higher prices caused by tariffs were passed along to the consumer, our great-grandparents, more-or-less. In this situation, they were paying the bulk of the revenue and those who were importing the stuff simply got rich. So Congress, in a compassionate gesture mind you, decided to tax everyone. This let them free to lower tariffs which should have resulted in lower costs for grandma and grandpa.

1913 is the year that our Federal Income Tax was installed (collecting began in 1914) and a small table is coming up that lets us compare trivia from a few of the last hundred years worth of income tax. Something that is not in the table is the Federal Budget.

The Federal budget is created by both the Executive and Legislative branches of the United States Federal Government. Our focus is on Congress but the responsibility for the Budget is shared with the President. It's involved, complicated and convoluted and because it's involved, complicated and convoluted I'll take the liberty of whittling it down a tad. In a nutshell, the President submits a budget proposal to Congress, Congress fiddles with it and voila, we have a budget unless somebody gets a burr under his saddle and decides to effectively shutdown the government. But I digress... wait a minute, I don't digress, I'm actually back on point.

The Federal Budget therefore is not part of the table. Besides, it's a shopping list, the nuts and bolts are in a few other details.

There are three columns in this table: the What, the How Much Was it Then, and the How Much Would That Be in 2013 either as a dollar amount adjusted for inflation or as a percentage of whatever is current.

Federal Corporate Income Tax
It would be unfair to say that corporations are not paying their share of the Federal Income Tax without knowing a few other things. Sure, there's more than one that lists its corporate office as a post office box in Ireland but that's most likely driven by globally competitive tax rates. Hmmm, there's a book. I wonder if Congress has anything to do with that? Globally competitive Corporate Taxation, I mean, hmmm. I wonder if we could experience any kind of growth at all if we could entice foreign companies into setting up their headquarters in the United States because our corporate tax rates were lower than their own countries. Hmmm. Of course, there are also those pesky State taxes to deal with.

Federal Individual Income Tax
How much our Federal Government made strictly from Individual Federal Income Tax.

Federal Income
All the money the Federal Government took in from taxes, fines, fees, whatever.

Federal Spending
How much the Federal Government spent.

Federal Surplus or Deficit
How much the Federal Government did not spend of the money they had or, more often than not, how much they overspent.

National Debt
> Add up all those Deficits that were never paid off and this is what you get or as I like to put it, All Those Unpaid Bills. I was going to call this the 'Federal Debt' but 'National Debt' is more accurate.

Population
> The population then and how that compares with the population in 2013. For instance, the population in 1914 was approximately 99,111,00 which is about 31% of the population in 2013.

Individual Income Tax Payers
> The number of Individual Federal Income Tax payers.

Percentage of Individual Income Tax Payers
> The percentage of the Population who paid Federal Income Tax.

Income Tax Payer Burden
> The percentage of the Total Federal Revenue that came from Individual Income Tax Payers: Total Federal Individual Income Tax ÷ Total Federal Income.

Individual Tax Burden
> This would be the tax if it was evenly divided between every man, woman and child of the United States.

Income Tax Payer Average
> The average Individual Federal Income Tax: Total Individual Federal Income Tax ÷ Total Individual Federal Income Tax Payers.

Individual National Debt Burden

We hire people to manage our Federal Money, we'll call them the Executive and Legislative branches of Government. They collect it, they invest it, they spend it but at the end of the day we're the ones who pick up the bill. The Individual National Debt Burden is the National Debt divided equally between every man, woman and child who is a U.S. Citizen so if you're part of a family of four you just go right ahead and multiply that number by four and that's what your family owes.

1913

	The Year 1913	What that looks like in 2013
Federal Corporate Income Tax	$0	$0
Federal Individual Income Tax	$0	$0
Federal Income	$344,424,453.85	$8,200,582,234.52
Federal Spending	$715,000,000.00	$17,023,809,523.81
Federal Deficit	Less Than $500,000.00	$11,904,761.90
National Debt	$2,916,204,913.66	$69,433,450,325.24
Population	97,225,000	30.75%
Federal Individual Income Tax Payers	0	0
Percentage of Individual Income Tax Payers	0%	
Income Tax Payer Burden	0%	
Individual Tax Burden	$3.54	$84.29
Individual Income Tax Payer Average	$0	$0
Individual National Debt Burden	$29.44	$700.95

1914

	The Year 1914	What that looks like in 2013
Federal Corporate Income Tax	$32,456,662.67	$754,806,108.60
Federal Individual Income Tax	$28,253,534.85	$657,058,950.00
Federal Income	$380,008,893.96	$8,837,416,138.60
Federal Spending	$726,000,000.00	$16,883,720,930.23
Federal Deficit	Less Than $500,000.00	$11,627,906.98
National Debt	$2,916,204,913.66	$67,818,718,922.33
Population	99,111,000	31.35%
Individual Income Tax Payers	357,598	In 2012: .2%
Percentage of Individual Income Tax Payers	.3%	
Individual Income Tax Payer Burden	7%	
Individual Tax Burden	$3.83	$89.07
Individual Income Tax Payer Average	$79	$1,837.21
Individual National Debt Burden	$29.42	$684.19

THE BALANCE OF POWER

First, a little thing on governments in general. There are a lot of governments, and you can find them in the Central Intelligence Agency's World FactBook, and a lot of types of governments, too. You know, like monarchy, socialist, plutocracy, et cetera... but the ones I'm not going to ignore are Direct Democracy and Constitutional Republic which some people also call a Representative Democracy. The term 'Democracy' is usually understood to be a Direct Democracy and the term Republic is usually understood to be a Constitutional Republic.

DoT: Oligarchy. The Telegraph, a newspaper that is a fairly big deal in Britain has recently reported on a study (Testing Theories of American Politics: Elites, Interest Groups, and Average Citizens) from Princeton University and Northwestern University, a couple of universities that are fairly big deals over here. According to the article the U.S.A. is, in practice, an oligarchy. In summary, an oligarchy is where the Haves-A-Lot get their way and the Have-A-Little, Haves-Not-So-Much and Haves-Not-At-All don't get their way. Even when the, we'll just call them the Everybody-Else for short, think they are getting their way they're really just riding the coattails of the Haves-A-Lot.

DoT: Economic Elite Domination. The conclusion you reach when the bulk of "nearly 1,800 US policies enacted" between 1981 and 2001 favor the "economic elite and/or organised interests".

In a Direct Democracy, the citizens vote for everything. In a Constitutional Republic the citizens elect people to represent their interests in the government. The actions of those elected are subsequently tempered by a set of rules, in our case the Constitution of the United States of America. And on to the Balance of Power.

The United States has three branches of government:

The Executive Branch	President
The Legislative Branch	Congress
The Judicial Branch	Supreme Court

Simply put, the Legislative Branch writes the rules, the Executive Branch enforces the rules and the Judicial Branch figures out what the heck the rules mean and whether or not they're legitimate. There were probably a few times they should have done that before the Executive Branch and Legislative Branch thought the rules were okay.

Traditionally, what we are taught is that in our government power is shared equally between the Executive Branch, the Legislative Branch and the Judicial Branch.

Rubbish.

THE ROUNDABOUT

In elementary school there was a roundabout. A circular platform centered on a pole that we took turns spinning and jumping on. What a great analogy for the Balance of Power as there are more than a few children in government today.

Imagine, if you will, that instead of a pole in the center of the platform there sits a fulcrum and that fulcrum is the Supreme Court. On top of the platform are the Executive and Legislative branches which are represented by Uncle Sam, the States, and the Citizens (you and I).

Call them whatever you want, accuse them of whatever you like, but the Executive Branch and the Judicial Branch do not write the laws, Congress writes the laws. The President can say 'No' but Congress can still pass the law. And if a law is poorly written, ambiguous or in conflict with the Constitution or some other law then it is left to the Supreme Court to interpret the law or throw the law out. If you don't like the result you have to blame the cause and not the symptom: Congress.

Which brings us to the whole point of this exercise - that the effect of those laws is an increasingly large Federal Government, more power in the hands of the Federal Government, more money spent by the Federal Government, more taxes required by the Federal Government and our Roundabout looking decidedly out of kilter.

Because marijuana is so high, ironically, on everyone's list it makes an excellent hypothetical demonstration of power and money. Let's say a state, California, votes to legalize marijuana but our elected officials at the Federal level oppose it. No problem, they simply pop off and create legislation that criminalizes marijuana on a Federal level. That legislation has to be supported by action and so now money has to be spent on buildings, computers, cleaning supplies, paper, fuel, administrative personnel, Federal agents, background checks, salaries, training, weapons, ammunition, health care, pensions, and the list goes on and on. And remember, this is a nationwide effort so thank you, Missouri, for not only funding Federal policing of marijuana in California but in your state as well and the other forty-eight states, too, even though all those States have their own police and bureaucracy to deal with their own laws, just like you.

One way the Federal government grows is by the imposition of the will of our Federal Congress over the will of the State governments or in California's case more than likely a proposition passed via a direct vote so, really, the direct will of the people of California. In this case we see the scale tipping clearly away from the equality of Federal .vs. State .vs. Individual and towards the Federal Government.

This shifting balance of power hasn't changed with the legalization of marijuana in Colorado, either. It is consumed without fear of criminal sanction only via the laissez-faire of the Federal Government. More specifically, because one or two men, the U.S. Attorney General and/or the President, have decided not to pursue legal action against the participants. Until Congress changes the law, the mere swearing in of a new President could result in staggering action in Colorado by the Federal Government. Smoke'em if you've got'em... unless, of course, Congress decides to tax marijuana. We all know what would happen if they started to do that.

As the balance of power drifts to the Federal Government we have to wonder if the Individual is becoming insignificant and irrelevant. When I was a youngster, I was taught that the Federal Government's role, relative to the Individual, was to guarantee minimum rights and that, while the State Governments could not reduce those rights, they could increase those rights. Enter the Administrative Subpoena.

The Administrative Subpoena is a subpoena that requires no judge to sign off on it. Although there appears to be a conflict with the Fourth Amendment, Congress doesn't see it that way and so the Roundabout tips a little further which brings us back to 1789.

In 1789 James Madison submitted the Bill of Rights to Congress because of the fear that the Federal Government would become too strong and evolve into something a little less dependent on the law of the land.

1930

	The Year 1930	What that looks like in 2013
Federal Corporate Income Tax	$275,588,648.53	$3,881,530,260.99
Federal Individual Income Tax	$247,502,042.64	$3,485,944,262.54
Federal Income	$580,615,592.31	$8,177,684,398.73
Federal Spending	$3,320,000,000.00	$46,760,563,380.28
Federal Surplus	+$738,000,000.00	$10,394,366,197.18
National Debt	$16,185,309,831.43	$227,962,110,301.83
Population	123,076,741	38.93%
Individual Income Tax Payers	1,872,268	In 2012: 1.3%
Percentage of Individual Income Tax Payers	1.5%	
Individual Income Tax Payer Burden	43%	
Individual Tax Burden	$4.72	$66.48
Individual Income Tax Payer Average	$132.19	$1,861.83
Individual National Debt Burden	$131.51	$1,852.25

LEGISLATIVE DYSFUNCTION

DoT: Legislative Dysfunction. What you get when Congress is in session.

First of all, have you ever wondered if they are politicians or professional actors? Ever wondered why so many hold the podium the same way, use their hands the same way, look into the crowds in the same way? Because they've either been coached to do that or they've picked it up without really understanding what is going on. They hold the podium because hands without purpose are distracting to the audience, they regularly looked at both sides of the audience to create a bond with the audience, same thing when they hold a hand, an often flat hand mind you, out to either side towards a section.

That bond they are trying to create by way of verbal and visual queues is a form of control and it is exactly what you see in the movies. The next time you go to one feel your emotions, young Jedi. You're happy by design, sad by design and want a sequel by design. It's a bit like eating potato chips, I'm happy when I'm eating them, feel guilty because I ate them and sad because they're all gone.

DoT: Legislative Dichotomy. See Legislative Dysfunction.

Congress is populated by the Democrats, the Republicans and a few Independents. I prefer to think that the rigid left and the rigid right, entrenched as they are in their own myopic worlds, are like empty-headed magnets, each one stuck to its own ilk and repelling the other for no more reason than because they are exactly the same and when it comes to magnets, the head is invariably stuck to the tail. When you have enough Independents they generate a depolarizing effect as the members uncouple in frantic attempts to win support of legislation by influencing the ones most likely to vote for their bill, in other words, anyone but the other party. To rephrase, what's a guy to do when the opposition is no way, no why or no how going to support his legislation? Try the Not-So-Opposition!

COMMON FRAMES OF REFERENCE

DoT: Apples and Oranges. This is my apple this is my orange this makes a pie and this makes a... heck, nothing rhymes with orange.

Let's briefly look at that which has come to be known as Obamacare. Personally, I would have just changed the eligibility rules for Medicare and Medicaid and supplemented it with some kind of tax Whups! There's that word again! Despite my faux pas, or perhaps in spite of it, the reason for the rising cost of health insurance has been debated at nauseating length along with what to do about it. And the reason you have a debate about the rising cost of health insurance is that nobody knows the reason why health care costs are rising, at least nobody outside the health care industry. Were the exact factors known, the Patient Protection and Affordable Care Act might have been decidedly different.

Finding the reason for rising insurance costs is complicated and who do you ask? The patients blame the insurers, the insurance companies blame the hospitals, the hospitals blame the patients and the doctor's insurance rates are going up, too, so assigning a definitive reason is an exercise in futility unless you know how to look, and few know how to look better than financial auditors.

At this point it helps to visualize the medical system as a tree, a perfectly naked tree with a lot of branches stuck to the trunk. Leafless. And each branch of the tree is something medical like an ambulance, the hospital, the pharmaceutical manufacturers, the doctor, nurse, insurance company, cotton swabs, stethoscopes and a few hundred other things. But in our case, only the ones that commonly work together in the real world. And now we need a patient.

Let's call him John Brickel. We'll call him John Brickel because the likelihood of John Brickel suing himself for using his own name is pretty low.

So John pops into the hospital for something not too catastrophic because God forbid he jinxes himself, and a lot of specifics start to get involved. A specific hospital, a specific insurance company, specific doctors, specific pharmacies, specific drugs - but just the fun ones, specific hardware and software, etc... Collect all those specifics and you have a tree then go build a half-a-dozen or so other trees around the country and you have the makings of something that can be studied in an objective way. And they can really be studied by forensic auditors. A bunch of really good ones aught to be able to tell us all about costs, and not only costs, but who raised their fees and in what order were all those specifics raising their fees. And not only that, but whether or not all those tree branches were raising their fees in line with their costs.

THE ACLU .VS. THE NRA

OR IS IT THE ACLU AND THE NRA?

The Second Amendment states the following:

> "A well regulated Militia, being necessary to the security
> of a free State, the right of the people to keep and bear
> Arms, shall not be infringed."

There is a single overarching debate about this Amendment, that is, does it apply to individuals or to collective bodies we formally acknowledge to be militia. The American Civil Liberties Union has publicly taken the position that it is the latter though they may be reviewing that in light of the Supreme Court having taken the position that it is the former.

If we look at the context under which it was written we can see two things right away: (1) the National Guard was first called the State Militia and was organized in 1636 so when the Continental Congress said 'militia' the State Militia was almost certainly foremost on their minds as they were well aware of its importance to their cause and (2) our nascent Republic was cash strapped and we relied on volunteers not only to join the fight but to bring their own weapons. There was no assurance, none, that we would survive much less grow into the richest nation on the planet and the likelihood was that we were going to continue to be cash-strapped for some time and in need of people to bring their own guns.

In 1785, after the Revolution, after the Continental Congress, after the Bill of Rights, Thomas Jefferson sent a letter to his nephew and suggested the gun as the apex of exercise. You know, running, jumping, shooting a gun. And he was a good shot.

In 1804, the Vice President of the United States, Aaron Burr, engaged in a duel with Alexander Hamilton who knew Jefferson what with them being a couple of our Founding Fathers. I think you kinda hafta believe that they had no problem with gun ownership and were well aware that North America as a whole was not only festooned with things that could kill you but that

20

hunting likely was a necessary condition of survival in outlying areas.

So if owning a gun is a right then what is all the fuss about? Well, basically, nukes are bad.

DoT: Arms. No, not the ones attached to your shoulder and bear arms doesn't mean bare arms or bear arms... well, Grizzly Bear arms. Arms are weapons, plain and simple. 20,000 years ago they were rocks, spears and atlatls.

By definition, not only is a nuclear missile a weapon but so is that paring knife in your kitchen drawer. The NRA no more wants you to personally own a nuclear bomb any more than the ACLU wants to take away your tomato knife. What they are trying to do is find the line in the sand and figure out if it is in a different place in different places... locations... cities. However, for such stalwart champions of the Second Amendment and Civil Liberties, I'm sometimes curious to know where they were when brass knuckles, nunchuks and stilletos were banned.

DoT: The Squeaky Wheel. If I shout loudly enough then I must be right. If I make more noise than everyone else then it doesn't matter how many disagree with me, nobody else can *also* be right because, you know, there's never more than one way to do something. Nobody knows what's good for them except me and, really, the Federal Government exists only for me, people like me, and nobody else.

DoT: The Silent Majority rebuts.

Moving along...

ARGUMENT .VS. DEBATE, COMPROMISE .VS. COLLABORATION AND WHAT DO I DO WITH DISCUSSION?

DoT: Discussion:
> Yo man, how're they hanging?
> *Dude, they're sticking to my knees.*
> Wow, that sucks.
> *Yes, it does.*

DoT: Debate:
> Yo man, how are they hanging?
> *Dude, they're sticking to my knees.*
> That seems unlikely as you wouldn't tolerate standing so tall.
> *I beg to differ! I tolerate a variety of things such as Congressional Gridlock and National Debt. I think I can stand upright with them sticking to my knees.*

DoT: Argument:
> Yo man, how're they hanging?
> *WTF!? What business is it of yours, you sick $%&**

DoT: Compromise:
> Yo man, how're they hanging?
> *Dude, they're sticking to my knees.*
> That seems unlikely as you wouldn't tolerate standing so tall.
> *I beg to differ. I tolerate a variety of things, such as Congressional Gridlock, National Debt and repetitiveness. I think I can walk with them sticking to my knees.*
> Certainly, but not upright.
> *Agreed. I do think I might stoop a little.*

DoT: Collaboration:
> Yo, man, let's see how they're hanging.
> *Okay!*

What is the difference between compromise and collaboration? You could put Rocky and Bullwinkle in the White House during quiet times with a collaborative Congress.

COMPETITION

We've been competing since the Stone Ages. It's in our brains, it's in our blood and if it's not in our DNA it's certainly in our societal DNA. How old were you when you first competed? What was the first game you played? Hide-and-Go-Seek? Were you six years old? Five?

Physical Education was required in elementary school and high school and a lot of that was built out of games, races, and generally competitions of one sort or another. There were no discussion classes but there was a debate club. People compete because Mother Nature gave us a set of tools like she did every other creature on Earth and it was up to our ancestors to live or die. Mother Nature can be an absolute bitch but we walked off and competed for food and for shelter, we survived and we compete to this day. We *run* for office, we *win* a seat in Congress. When candidates are debating the one who wins the debate doesn't win because his idea was any better than anyone else's. He wins because he has imposed himself over everyone else. His ideas win because he was better at imposing them. People win because of an imposition of will.

To look at this another way, in sports, say football or baseball or anyball, an athlete rises through the collegiate ranks and earns a spot on a professional team not because he is better at talking the coaches into thinking he's the best pick, on the contrary, he earns the position because he has demonstrated that he is better at the job than any other available candidate. A politician, on the other hand, wins an election because he is better at talking the voter into thinking that he is a better candidate, no other skill set is required. Frame this in the context of competition and what you have are a Congress chock-full of Representatives and Senators who are better at competing in an election than anyone they had met before without any demonstrative requirement that they are better at the skills required in the job than anyone else. And there they are, quintessential competitors, staring across the aisles at one another, daring those brains attached to those eyeballs to cross the Rubicon.

DoT: Argument. How often has a conversation turned into a debate that turned into an argument? Lots. An argument is a competition, it is a single-minded effort to impose one will over another.

If an Idiot Runs for Congress and We Vote for the Idiot, is it the Idiot's Fault if He Wins?

DoT: Idiots. I'm not referring to people who are in some way or another more intellectually challenged than the rest of us. By idiots, I mean men (there's that gender thing again, or lack thereof) who should know better but who make decisions that cause us to question their intellectual capacity to suss facts and truth and work in a productive way or, contrarily, that make us believe they are acting stupidly, egocentrically or lazily. For example, let's talk gambling.

On any given roulette table, the odds of getting a red is slightly less than fifty percent because, even though there are the same number of red and black pockets, the addition of the green pocket or two puts the odds in the house's favor. Now, if a person makes eighty thousand dollars a year, has no debt and once in a blue moon wants to go to a roulette table and put a hundred dollars on red, he has slightly less than a 50% chance of winning and that is fun, exciting and no big deal. On the other hand, if a guy is a displaced worked, has five thousand in the bank, takes the deed to his paid-for house and puts it on red then he has a slightly more than 50% chance of losing and we might think of him as an idiot.

At this point many of you might automatically think that this is eerily similar to a member of congress spearheading a shutdown. After all, the odds are not in his favor and he is gambling with the income of many people who are trying to pay for food or rent or mortgages on their homes and essentially costing the economy between three and twenty-four billion dollars, or so, depending on what you read. You would be wrong, however, because he was not gambling with his money, he was gambling with yours.

It is fair to say that there are people in both Houses of Congress who work hard, take their jobs very seriously, and who think of themselves as having been hired by their constituency. It is also fair to say that there are people in both Houses of

Congress with Napoleonic egos. If a person demonstrates, on the campaign trail for instance, a propensity for bullying, for self-aggrandizement, for an unwillingness to confront issues in a sane and logical way, for being unable or unwilling to explore avenues of cooperation with the opposition or even compromise with the opposition and if he behaves the same way after being elected... whose fault is that?

DoT: Discussion. Discussion creates an oasis where thoughtful dialogue replaces rhetoric, where common ground can be discovered and a place from which those participants can leave in complete and utter disagreement but with a knowledge and understanding of each other's perspective. In short, it is an opportunity to find those Definitions of Terms and Common Frames of Reference and dissect issues and solutions without being tainted by extremist views. It is an island in the maelstrom of Congress. Surely it goes on in their corridors everyday... it would be helpful, however, if it were a bigger island so the rest of us could see it from time-to-time.

1950

	The Year 1950	What that looks like in 2013
Federal Corporate Income Tax	$10,854,351,109.00	$105,382,049,601.94
Federal Individual Income Tax	$17,153,307,948.00	$166,536,970,368.93
Federal Income	$28,007,659,057.00	$271,919,019,970.87
Federal Spending	$42,562,000,000.00	$413,223,300,970.87
Federal Deficit	$3,100,000,000.00	$30,097,087,378.64
National Debt	$257,357,352,351.04	$2,498,615,071,369.32
Population	152,271,417	48.16%
Individual Income Tax Payers	51,841,335	In 2012: 36%
Percentage of Individual Income Tax Payers	34%	
Individual Income Tax Payer Burden	61%	
Individual Tax Burden	$183.93	$1,785.73
Individual Income Tax Payer Average	$330.88	$3,212.43
Individual National Debt Burden	$1,690.12	$16,408.93

ANALYSIS AND LOGIC

We talked about BETTER! in the introduction but let's raise the bar a little and look at profits on a gallon of gasoline.

Scenario Number 1: Hypothetically, let's say an oil company gets a 10% profit per gallon of gas and gas costs $1. I know, the glaze is already going over your eyes but I promise this will be easy. In this case it's in the best interest of the oil company for the price of a gallon of gas to be as high as possible because at $1 their profit is 10 cents, at $2 per gallon their profit is 20 cents, at $3 per gallon it's 30 cents and so forth.

Scenario Number 2: Hypothetically, let's say that same oil company only gets a fixed amount of profit per gallon, we'll make it 10 cents. Not 10% just 10 centavos. In this case, it's in the best interest of the gas company for the price of gas to be as little as possible so that more gas will be consumed because no matter what price a gallon of gasoline is, be it $1 or $2 or $5, they will only get 10 cents per gallon.

Popping off to the American Petroleum Institute's website (Appendix B, References) there is a summary report of taxes on gasoline by State. There is also a disclaimer to the effect that we cannot be absolutely sure it is accurate given the volatile (get it?) nature of gas taxation around the country. Right now, however, the Federal Tax is 18.4 cents per gallon meaning that it would be in Congress' best interest for gas to be as inexpensive as possible. Of course, Congress is also taxing the companies that are profiting from the sale of that gallon of gas and, if they do what they do with me and probably you then they do this by charging the companies tax as a percentage. Simply put, that would be Congress betting both horses in a two-horse race.

The following page illustrates how it is that the price of gas has managed to keep going up.

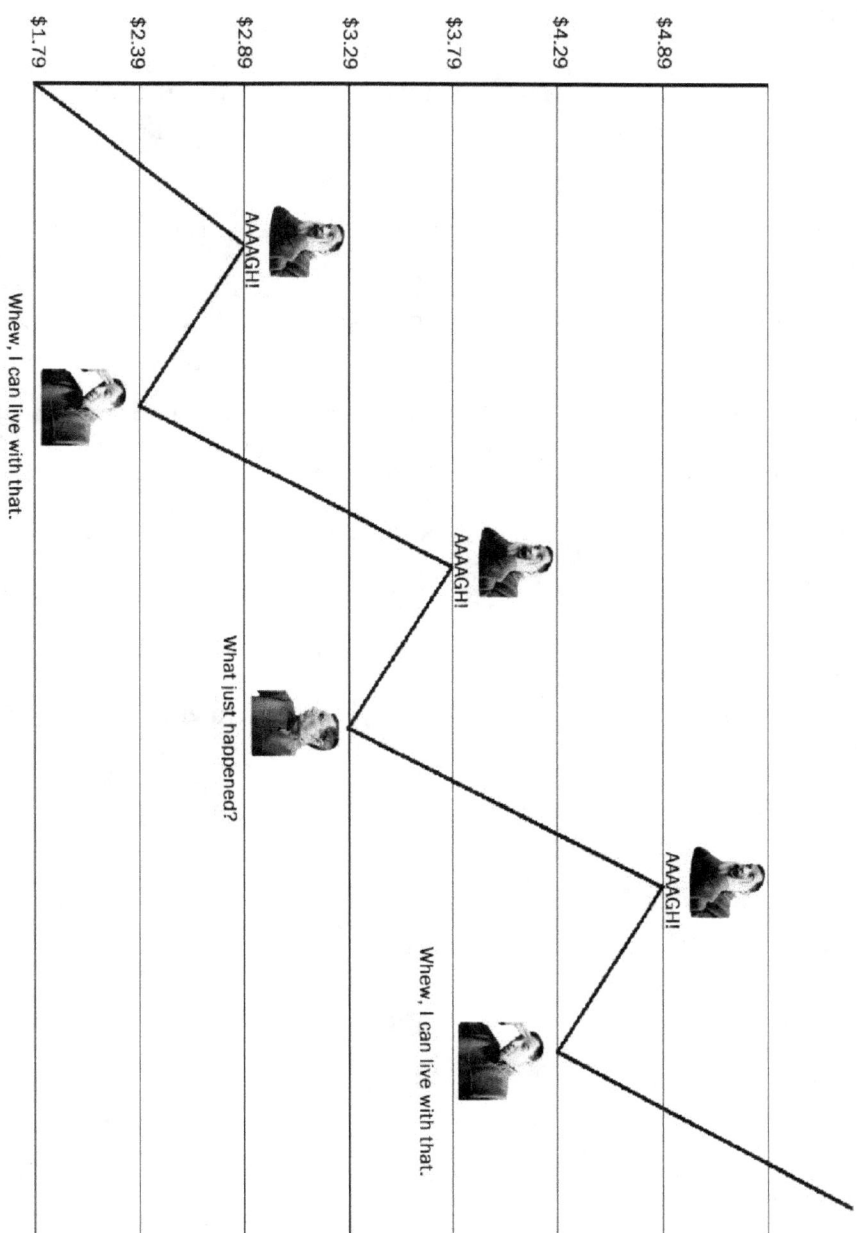

1970

	The Year 1970	What that looks like in 2013
Federal Corporate Income Tax	$35,036,983,000.00	$211,066,162,650.60
Federal Individual Income Tax	$103,651,585,000.00	$624,407,138,554.22
Federal Income	$195,722,096,000.00	$1,179,048,771,084.34
Federal Spending	$195,649,000,000.00	$1,178,608,433,734.94
Federal Deficit	$2,800,000,000.00	$16,867,469,879.52
National Debt	$370,918,706,949.93	$2,234,450,041,867.05
Population	205,052,174	64.85%
Individual Income Tax Payers	78,370,000	In 2012: 55%
Percentage of Individual Income Tax Payers	38%	
Individual Income Tax Payer Burden	53%	
Individual Tax Burden	$954.50	$5,750.00
Individual Income Tax Payer Average	$1,322.59	$7,967.41
Individual National Debt Burden	$1,808.90	$10,896.99

POLICY ENTREPRENEURS

The term 'entrepreneur' in the context of government has been slowly entering our vernacular. Mostly it is a part of a term, such as 'political entrepreneur' or 'policy entrepreneur' or some other slick sounding whatever in front of 'entrepreneur'.

DoT: Policy Entrepreneur. There are several definitions of Policy Entrepreneur but let's use the inferred, implied or largely unspoken one: a Policy Entrepreneur is someone who seeks to create or change legislation for his own ends.

Having defined a Policy Entrepreneur, let me continue by saying that 'his own ends' might be completely altruistic and for a decidedly common purpose. They might also be for personal or political gain. In any case, the question becomes: is the policy being pursued in the National Interest?

By definition Congressmen have divided interests: the National Interest and their own Regional Interest and doing something in the National Interest might not necessarily win you votes back home. Nevertheless, they are spending National money so it seems reasonable to expect it would be employed in the National Interest. Of course, now we have to figure out what 'National Interest' means.

Intuitively, it is in the National Interest for a poverty stricken State to be helped because that would increase the number of contributors - those would be tax paying, idea formulating, job creating contributors which always helps us as a whole because those contributions make that State more competitive and they can then turn around and help another less fortunate State. Some of those ideas can, in fact, directly make our entire Nation more competitive.

Also intuitively, something that would not be in the National Interest would be a Bridge-to-Nowhere in the middle of an oil rich State, let's say Alaska or, and I'm winging it here, a Federal Shutdown spurred by Policy Entrepreneurs.

The Federal Shutdown of 2013 is often looked at as a failed effort to control policy in favor of a particular political movement but if we apply our definition of Policy Entrepreneur it becomes necessary to ask how it might have been a success. It could arguably be looked at as a success if the objective had been to make someone widely known, it can probably be considered a success if the objective had been to seal a relationship with a particular political segment. It is hard to look past, however, the impact to those in need and the marginalization of the alluded to political segment. (*For the record: this author has no knowledge of or, frankly, any interest whatsoever in the actual motivation for the effort that resulted in the Federal Government Shutdown of 2013, only the effect of that effort relative to the stated definition.*)

It's not fair, of course, to keep picking on one event but it conveniently illustrates activities that, while not as grand in scale, seem to go on with more frequency, more subtlety and with their own particular effect.

1980

	The Year 1980	What that looks like in 2013
Federal Corporate Income Tax	$72,379,610,000.00	$205,623,892,045.45
Federal Individual Income Tax	$287,547,782,000.00	$816,897,107,954.55
Federal Income	$519,375,273,000.00	$1,475,497,934,659.09
Federal Spending	$590,941,000,000.00	$1,678,809,659,090.91
Federal Deficit	$73,830,000,000.00	$209,744,318,181.82
National Debt	$907,701,000,000.00	$2,578,696,022,727.27
Population	227,224,681	71.87%
Individual Income Tax Payers	107,827,000	In 2012: 75%
Percentage of Individual Income Tax Payers	47%	
Individual Income Tax Payer Burden	55%	
Individual Tax Burden	$2,285.73	$6,493.55
Individual Income Tax Payer Average	$2,666.75	$7,575.99
Individual National Debt Burden	$3,994.73	$11,348.66

35

TAXES

I'm going to start this with an actual quote from an IRS publication entitled 'The Complexity of the Tax Code'. It was written by the Taxpayer Advocate Service and is part of its 2008 Annual Report to Congress.

> "The most serious problem facing taxpayers is the complexity of the Internal Revenue Code."

Small wonder. In 2006 the United States Federal Tax Code was around 67,000 pages. In 2010 it was approaching 72,000 pages. In 2013 it was just shy of 74,000 pages. Gee, I sense a pattern here. It's really well worth reading this document (not the code - BORING, the publication). Here are a few fun facts from it:

> Since 2001 there have been more than 3,250 changes.

> In 1975 the Tax Code was 1,395,000 words but by 2008 it was up to 3,700,000 words.

> In 2006, the cost of complying with the tax code - that's not paying taxes, that's the money we paid to make sure we were paying taxes - was $193,000,000,000. (I could have said $193 billion, but typing all those zeroes is kind of meditative.)

There are plenty of other gems like the ones above but my favorite extract from the document is this:

> "The Code contains no comprehensive Taxpayer Bill of Rights that explicitly and transparently sets out taxpayer rights and obligations. Taxpayers do have rights, but they are scattered throughout the Code and the Internal Revenue Manual and are neither easily accessible nor written in plain language that most taxpayers can understand."

This document is a gift to us all. It is not long, it is loaded with salient points, thoughtful critique and reasonable recommendations, and it is worth a read. And if you don't know by now, we have a National Taxpayer Advocate. We should all know the Taxpayer Advocate Service exists and how to contact it. They have a video, too. For that and details about "The Complexity of the Tax Code" Please see Appendix B, References.

DoT: Taxes. Taxes are taxes be they called Income, Excise, Surtax, Gift, Duty, Toll, Fee, Fine, etc... Seriously, did you really think Congress was happy with just your Income Tax?

SALES TAX VERSUS FEDERAL INCOME TAX

The immediate difference between a sales tax and an Federal Income Tax is that with the sales tax everyone pays whether they are a U.S. Citizen, tourist, or immigrant - legal or otherwise. With a Federal Income Tax, the burden is entirely on the Federal Income Tax payer. Thus, and depending on the tax threshold, in the former situation it is in the best interest of the Nation to have a large population of purchasers while in the latter it is in the best interest of the individual taxpayer to have as few people as possible sharing the road - by which I mean, to have as few people as possible utilizing goods and services paid for via the Federal Income Tax.

Today, for example, the Federal Income Tax paying Citizens of Missouri graciously pay the Department of Homeland Security (DHS) to ensure that tourists from France and a hundred or so other countries can safely fly into New York and then onto California or Florida to spend their money at Disneyland... or World... or Disney... whatever. Pick a theme park, golf course or any spot along thousands of miles of beaches. Sigh. The sound spilling out of my lips is only a wisp of nostalgia as I write this in the shadow of New York City, looking out my window at the snow-encrusted ground of New Jersey and watching the ice float down the Hudson. But I digress. In the former situation, the more people that come to the U.S. the more the burden is removed from any individual taxpayer.

Of course, it's particularly good for New York, California and Florida who are the principal recipients of those jobs and those tourists. I'm from Florida, sigh, which does not have a State Income Tax, sigh, but does have an awful lot of tourists and I think I can speak for many Floridians when I say thanks you Citizens of Missouri and all you Citizens of all those other States out there!

Still, life has its symmetry. The first thing to know about the United States Federal Income Tax is that it can be offset, to some degree, by the tax you pay to your State, at least, in the States I've been in. I hope so or my accountant screwed up royally. Therefore, if you live in Alaska, Florida, Nevada, South Dakota, Texas, or Washington, you are paying a disproportionately higher Federal tax than residents of the other forty-four States.

DoT: Loophole. The effect of a law written in such a way as to allow itself to be legally skirted. With 72,000 pages you'd think they had it covered but evidently not. It does makes one wonder how many pages are dedicated to closing loopholes.

1990

	The Year 1990	What that looks like in 2013
Federal Corporate Income Tax	$93,133,625,000.00	$166,607,558,139.53
Federal Individual Income Tax	$463,441,656,000.00	$829,054,840,787.12
Federal Income	$959,114,855,000.00	$1,715,768,971,377.46
Federal Spending	$1,252,994,000,000.00	$2,241,491,949,910.55
Federal Deficit	$221,036,000,000.00	$395,413,237,924.87
National Debt	$3,233,313,451,777.25	$5,784,102,775,987.93
Population	249,464,396	78.91%
Individual Income Tax Payers	112,492,000	In 2012: 78%
Percentage of Individual Income Tax Payers	45%	
Individual Income Tax Payer Burden	48%	
Individual Tax Burden	$3,844.70	$6,877.82
Individual Income Tax Payer Average	$4,119.77	$7,369.89
Individual National Debt Burden	$12,961.02	$23,186.08

BUREAUCRACIES

It isn't all Social Security, Medicare and Medicaid, Welfare, and the Military, you know. They're just a few of the big ones and they aren't responsible for all of the spending or growth of the Federal Government. You could call it a symptom of Federal growth or you could say that the rubber meets the road in the number of agencies of the United States Federal Government. What follows is a partial list of agencies that appear in the U.S. government website, USA.gov, that was created for our informational purposes.

As you browse this list, keep in mind that each agency likely requires support of one kind or another such as supplies, janitorial services, accounting services, website services, they may require transportation, telecommunications, a building, electricity, and a host of other services that exist only to support them and which have nothing to do with their purpose, per se. In short, one line of ink on a piece of paper and the price of running the government goes up.

This information was gotten from English language Wikipedia articles, directly from the agency's website or the National Archives. I stuck to Wikipedia in most cases because I was paranoid about being hauled away and interrogated because of my interest in all those Federal Government agencies, even though everything is in the public domain and I only wanted dates of origin. Some world we live in, huh?

Some of these agencies grew out of ideas and institutions that were framed before their actual establishment. Since the modern day agency was the inevitable outcome of these it seemed more appropriate to give credit where credit was due so the date of the root of the agency is listed to the left. Under the name is the evolution of the agency.

1600s & 1700s

Historical
Beginning
or
Precedent **Agency**

1.   1636   National Guard
        1636: est. State Militias
        1916: renamed National Guard
        1933: est. State/Federal Reserve Forces

2.   1772   United States Postal Inspection Service
        1772: Benjamin Franklin, Postmaster General, appoints Mails Surveyor
        1801: renamed Special Agent
        1830: est. Office of Instructions and Mail Depredations
        1880: 'Special Agent; renamed 'Inspector'

3.   1774   Congress - U.S. House of Representatives
        Sept 5, 1774: The First Continental Congress
        1787: Constitutional Convention
        1788: Constitution ratified
        1789: First Convened

4.   1774   Congress - U.S. Senate
        Sept 5, 1774: The First Continental Congress
        1787: Constitutional Convention
        1788: Constitution ratified
        1789: First Convened

5.   1775   U.S. Army

		1775: Continental Army
		1784: United States Army officially created
6.	1775	U.S. Army Corps of Engineers
		1779: established as a separate Corps
7.	1775	U.S. Marine Corps
8.	1775	U.S. Postal Service (USPS)
9.	1776	U.S. Department of Veterans Affairs (VA)
		1776: Continental Congress est. pensions for disabled soldiers
		1811: authorization for Philadelphia Naval Asylum
		1917: est. Veterans Bureau, Bureau of Pensions, National Home for Disabled Volunteer Soldiers
		1930: est. Veterans Administration
10.	1787	House of Representatives
		1787: Constitutional Convention
		1788: Constitution Ratified
		1789: House in session
11.	1787	White House
		1787: Constitutional Convention
		1788: Constitution ratified
		1789: George Washington
12.	1778	U.S. Military Academy, West Point
		1778: est. Army Post
		1794: est. training in Artillery and Engineering
		1802 est. United States Military Academy
13.	1789	Bureau of Customs and Border Protection
		1789: est. U.S. Customs Service
		2003: est. Bureau of Customs and Border Protection
14.	1789	Department of Defense
		1789: est. War Department
		1798: est. Navy Department
		1947: National Military Establishment created from Departments of War and

Navy

1949: renamed Department of Defense

15.	1789	Department of Justice

1789: est. Attorney General

1870: est. Department of Justice

16.	1789	Judicial Circuit Courts of Appeal
17.	1789	Office of the Clerk, U.S. House of Representatives
18.	1789	Supreme Court of the United States
19.	1789	U.S. Circuit Courts of Appeal
20.	1789	U.S. Department of State
21.	1789	U.S. Department of the Treasury
22.	1789	U.S. Immigration and Customs Enforcement

1789: est. U.S. Customs Service

2003: est. Immigration and Customs Enforcement Division

23.	1789	U.S. Marshals Service

1789: Judiciary Act

1965: est. Executive Office for U.S. Marshals

1969: Marshals Service

24.	1790	Copyright Office
25.	1790	U.S. Coast Guard

1790: est. Revenue Marine

1860: known as U.S. Revenue Cutter Service

1848: est. U.S. Life-Saving Service

1915: est. U.S. Coast Guard by merger of RCC and LSS

26.	1790	U.S. Patent and Trademark Office
27.	1792	United States Mint
28.	1793	Architect of the Capitol
29.	1798	U.S. Department of Health and Human Services

1798: est. Marine Hospital Service

1902: Public Health and Marine Hospital Service

1912: renamed Public Health Service

1921: est. Bureau of Indian Affairs

Health Division
1939: est. Federal Security Agency
1946: est. Communicable Disease
Center
1953: est. Department of Health,
Education and Welfare (Cabinet-level)
1965: est. Medicare and Medicaid
1970: est. National Health Service
Corps
1977: est. Health Care Financing
Administration
1980: est. Department of Health and
Human Services

30.   1790   U.S. Navy
1790: U.S. Revenue Cutter Service
1794: Congress orders six frigates
1797: launched USS United States, USS
Constellation, USS Constitution

1800s

31.	1800	Library of Congress
32.	1801	U.S. Capitol Police
33.	1812	Bureau of Land Management (BLM)

                    1812: est. General Land Office
                    1937: est. Grazing Service
                    1946: General Land Office merges with the Grazing Service to form the BLM

34.	1824	Bureau of Indian Affairs (BIA)
35.	1825	Defense Commissary Agency
36.	1830	National Institute of Standards and Technology

                    1830: est. Office of Standard Weights and Measures
                    1901: est. National Bureau of Standards
                    1988: renamed National Institute of Standards and Technology

37.	1834	Armed Forces Retirement Home

                    1834: est. U.S. Naval Home
                    1851: est. U.S. Soldiers' and Airmen's Home
                    1991: est. Armed Forces Retirement Home

38.	1838	Federal Mediation and Conciliation Service

                    1838: federally mediated shipyard workers strike
                    1918: est. U.S. Conciliation Service
                    1947: est. Federal Mediation and Conciliation Service

39.	1839	Department of Agriculture

                    1839: Agricultural Division of Patent Office
                    1862: Department of Agriculture

40.	1840	Bureau of the Census

                    Prior to 1840, the census was the responsibility of the Justice Department

41.	1846	Smithsonian Institution

| 42. | 1849 | Department of the Interior (DOI) |
| 43. | 1849 | Bureau of Safety and Environmental Enforcement |

        1849: est. Department of Interior
        1879: est. U.S. Geological Survey
        1982, est. Minerals Management Service
        2010: est. Bureau of Safety and Environmental Enforcement

| 44. | 1849 | Bureau of Ocean Energy Management |

        1849: est. Department of Interior
        1879: est. U.S. Geological Survey
        1982, est. Minerals Management Service
        2010: est. Bureau of Ocean Energy Management

| 45. | 1849 | Office of Natural Resources Revenue |

        1849: est. Department of Interior
        1879: est. U.S. Geological Survey
        1982, est. Minerals Management Service
        2010: est. Office of Natural Resources Revenue

| 46. | 1850 | U.S. Botanic Garden |
| 47. | 1855 | Court of Appeals for the Federal Circuit |

        1855: est. Court of Claims, 1948: renamed to U.S. Court of Claims
        1909: est. U.S. Court of Customs and Patent Appeals
        1982: est. via merger of the U.S. Court of Claims and the U.S. Court of Customs and Patent Appeals

| 48. | 1855 | Court of Federal Claims |

        1855: est. Court of Claims
        1948: renamed United States Court of Claims
        1982: replaced by United States Claims Court
        1992: renamed United States Court of

Federal Claims
49.   1860   Government Printing Office (GPO)
50.   1861   Bureau of Engraving and Printing
              1861: Secretary of Treasury prints
              paper currency
              1863: est. Office of Comptroller of the
              Currency and National Currency
              Bureau
              1874: est. Bureau of Engraving and
              Printing
51.   1862   Center for Food Safety and Applied Nutrition
              1862: est. Division of Chemistry
              1901: est. Bureau of Chemistry
              1906: Food and Drug Act
              1927: est. Food, Drug, and Insecticide
              Organization (FDIO)
              1930: FDIO renamed Food and Drug
              Administration
              1984: est. Center for Food Safety and
              Applied Nutrition
52.   1862   Food Safety and Inspection Service
              1862: est. U.S. Department of
              Agriculture
              1884: est. Bureau of Animal Industry
              1887: Interstate Commerce Act
              1901: est. Bureau of Chemistry (BoC)
              1906: Pure Food and Drug Act
              1906: Federal Meat Inspection Act
              1927: BoC renamed Food, Drug and
              Insecticide Administration (FDIA)
              1931: FDIA renamed Food and Drug
              Administration
              1953: est. Agricultural Research Service
              1971: est. Animal and Plant Health
              Service
              1977: est. Food Safety and Quality
              Service (FSQS)
              1981: FSQS renamed Food Safety and
              Inspection Service

53.	1862	Internal Revenue Service (IRS)
		1862: est. Commissioner of Internal Revenue
		1894: est. Bureau of Internal Revenue
		1953: renamed Internal Revenue Service
54.	1862	National Cemetery Administration (NCA)
		1862: Congress authorizes expenditure for creation of national cemeteries for veterans
		1973: consolidated into National Cemetery System
		1998: renamed National Cemetery Administration
55.	1865	Secret Service
56.	1870	National Weather Service (NOAA)
		1870: est. Weather Bureau of the United States
		1970: renamed National Weather Service
57.	1871	Fish and Wildlife Service
		1871: est. United States Commission on Fish and Wildlife
		1885: est. Division of Economic Ornithology and Mammalogy (DEOM)
		1896: renamed DEOM Division of Biological Survey
		1940: est. Fish and Wildlife Service
58.	1871	National Marine Fisheries Service
		1871: est. U.S. Commission of Fish and Fisheries
		currently known as National Marine Fisheries Service
59.	1876	Forest Service
		1876: est. Office of Special Agent (Dept. of Agriculture)
		1881: Division of Forestry
		1901: renamed Bureau of Forestry
60.	1879	Mississippi River Commission

| 61. | 1879 | U.S. Geological Survey (USGS) |
| 62. | 1882 | Foreign Agricultural Service |

        1882: USDA posts Statistical Agent in London

        1930: est. Foreign Agricultural Service

| 63. | 1883 | Office of Personnel Management (OPM) |

        1883: est. U.S. Civil Service Commission

        1972: est. Office of Personnel Management

64.	1884	Bureau of Labor Statistics
65.	1863	Office of the Comptroller of the Currency (OCC)
66.	1886	Alcohol and Tobacco Tax and Trade Bureau

        1886: est. Revenue Laboratory

        1920: est. Bureau of Internal Revenue

        1933: est. Alcohol Tax Unit (ATU)

        1950: (circa) ATU renamed Alcohol and Tobacco Tax Division

        1968: renamed Alcohol, Tobacco and Firearms Division

        1972: est. Bureau of Alcohol, Tobacco and Firearms

        2003: est. Alcohol, Tobacco Tax and Trade Bureau

| 67. | 1886 | Bureau of Alcohol, Tobacco, Firearms, and Explosives |

        1886: est. Revenue Laboratory

        1920: est. Bureau of Internal Revenue

        1933: est. Alcohol Tax Unit (ATU)

        1950: (circa) ATU renamed Alcohol and Tobacco Tax Division

        1968: renamed Alcohol, Tobacco and Firearms Division

        1972: est. Bureau of Alcohol, Tobacco and Firearms

        2002: est. Bureau of Alcohol Tobacco, Firearms and Explosives

| 68. | 1887 | National Institutes of Health (NIH) |

		1887: est. Hygienic Laboratory
		1922: renamed Public Health Services
		1930: renamed National Institutes of Health
69.	1889	Department of Labor (DOL)
70.	1890	Antitrust Division
		1890: Sherman Antitrust Act
		1933: est. Antitrust Division
71.	1890	U.S. Court of International Trade
		1890: est. Board of General Appraisers
		1926: est. U.S. Customs Court
		1980: renamed U.S. Court of International Trade
72.	1891	U.S. Citizenship and Immigration Services
		1891: Commissioner of Immigration
		1938: est. Immigration and Naturalization Service
		2003: est. U.S. Citizenship and Immigration Service
73.	1893	Federal Highway Administration
		1893: est. Office of Road Inquiry
		1905: renamed Office of Public Roads
		1915: renamed Bureau of Public Roads
		1939: renamed Public Roads Administration
		1966: est. Federal Highway Administration (FHA)
		1967: FHA assumes the responsibilities of the Public Roads Administration
74.	1898	U.S. Trustee Program
		1898: Bankruptcy Act
		1938: Bankruptcy Act
		1978: Bankruptcy Reform Act

75.	1901	Joint Congressional Committee on Inaugural Ceremonies
76.	1902	Bureau of Reclamation
77.	1903	Commerce Department
78.	1903	U.S. Department of Commerce (DOC)

> 1903: est. U.S. Department of Commerce and Labor
> 1913: renamed Department of Commerce

| 79. | 1903 | Joint Chiefs of Staff |

> 1903: est. Joint Army and Navy Board
> 1942 est. Joint Chiefs of Staff

| 80. | 1906 | Food and Drug Administration (FDA) |

> (1848: est. lab for agricultural chemical analysis)
> (1862, est. U.S. Department of Agriculture)
> 1906: Food and Drug Act
> 1927: Bureau of Chemistry
> 1930: renamed Food and Drug Administration

| 81. | 1908 | Federal Bureau of Investigation (FBI) |

> 1908: est. Bureau of Investigation
> 1932: renamed United States Bureau of Investigation
> 1935: renamed Federal Bureau of Investigation

| 82. | 1909 | Office of Fossil Energy |

> 1909: est. Naval Petroleum and Oil Shale Reserves
> 1918: est. Bartlesville Experiment Station
> 1961: est. Office of Coal Research
> 1974: est. Energy Research and Development Administration
> 1975: est. U.S. Strategic Petroleum Reserve

		1977: est. Department of Energy
		1979: est. Office of Fossil Energy
83.	1910	U.S. Commission of Fine Arts
84.	1910	U.S. Department of Energy National Laboratories

This is a system of national labs, currently numbering seventeen. The oldest appears to be the National Energy Technology Laboratory at Pittsburgh, Pennsylvania.

| 85. | 1913 | Agricultural Marketing Service |

        1913: est. Office of Markets
        1922: est. Bureau of Agricultural Economics
        1939: est. Agricultural Marketing Service

| 86. | 1913 | Federal Reserve System |
| 87. | 1914 | Congressional Research Service |

        1914: est. unit of Library of Congress
        1946: renamed Legislative Reference Service
        1970: renamed Congressional Research Service

| 88. | 1914 | Federal Trade Commission (FTC) |
| 89. | 1916 | Federal Maritime Commission |

        1916: est. U.S. Shipping Board
        1933: est. U.S. Shipping Board Bureau
        1950: est. Federal Maritime Board
        1961: est. Federal Maritime Commission

| 90. | 1916 | Grain Inspection, Packers and Stockyards Administration |

        1916: est. national grain inspection system
        1921: est. Packers and Stockyards Administration
        1976: est. Grain Inspection, Packers and Stockyards Administration

| 91. | 1916 | National Park Service |
| 92. | 1916 | U.S. International Trade Commission |

1916: est. Tariff Commission
1974: renamed U.S. International
Trade Commission

93.   1917   National Security Agency (NSA)
1917: est. Cable and Telegraph Section
(MI-8),
*(Author's Note: I have attempted to establish
origins and iterations of various agencies in
this list so as to tie the credit for the modern
agency to its roots. The NSA has a veritable
plethora of branches in its tree and I would
encourage anyone interested in history to
explore the National Archives. Its address, as
well as one germane to this item, are in
Appendix B.)*
1952: est. National Security Agency

94.   1917   Selective Service System (SSS)
1917: Selective Service Act
1940: Selective Training and Service
Act
1948: Selective Service Act

95.   1920   Women's Bureau (Labor Department)
96.   1921   Government Accountability Office (GAO)

1921: est. General Accounting Office
2004: renamed Government
accountability Office

97.   1921   Office of Management and Budget (OMB)
1921: est. Bureau of the Budget
1970: renamed Office of Management
and Budget

98.   1922   Economic Research Service
1922: est. Bureau of Agricultural
Economics
1961: est. Economic Research Service

99.   1922   U.S. Commodity Futures Trading
Commission (CFTC)
1922: Grain Futures Act
1936: Commodity Exchange Act

		1974: Commodity Futures Trading Commission Act
100.	1923	American Battle Monuments Commission
101.	1924	Dwight D. Eisenhower School for National Security and Resource Strategy
		1924: est. Army Industrial College
		1946: renamed Industrial College of the Armed Forces
102.	1924	Industrial College of the Armed Forces
		1924: est. Army Industrial College
		1943: re-est. Army Industrial College
		1946: renamed Industrial College of the Armed Forces
103.	1924	National Capital Planning Commission
		1924: est. National Capital Park Commission
		1952: renamed National Capital Planning Commission
104.	1924	U.S. Tax Court
		1924: est. U.S. Board of Tax Appeals
		1942: renamed Tax Court of the United States
		1969: renamed U.S. Tax Court
105.	1926	National Transportation Safety Board
		1926: Air Commerce Act
		1938: Civil Aeronautics Act
		1938: est. Civil Aeronautics Authority
		1940: est. Civil Aeronautics Board
		1967: est. National Transportation Safety Board
106.	1927	U.S. National Arboretum
107.	1929	Migratory Bird Conservation Commission
108.	1929	Substance Abuse and Mental Health Services Administration
		1929: est. Narcotics Division, 1930: est. Division of Mental Hygiene
		1949: est. National Institutes of Health
		1968: Health Services and Mental Health Administration

		1973: re-est. National Institutes of Health
		1970: est. National Institute on Alcohol Abuse and Alcoholism
		1973: est. Alcohol, Drug Abuse, and Mental Health Administration
		1992: est. Substance Abuse and Mental Health Services Administration
109.	1930	Bureau of Prisons
110.	1930	Federal Energy Regulatory Commission
		1930: est. Federal Power Commission
		1977: renamed Federal Energy Regulatory Commission
111.	1930	Federal Bureau of Prisons
112.	1930	National Gallery of Art
		1930: Andrew W. Mellon est. A. W. Mellon Educational and Charitable Trust
		1937: Mellon donates art collection and building funds
		1937: est. National Gallery of Art, 1941: Open
113.	1933	Bureau of Citizenship and Immigration Services (USCIS)
		2003: Immigration and Naturalization Service transitioned into the USCIS
114.	1933	Farm Credit Administration
115.	1933	Farm Service Agency
		1933: Agricultural Adjustment Administration
		1943: War Food Administration
		1994: est. Farm Service Agency
116.	1933	National Labor Relations Board
		1933: National Industrial Recovery Act
		1933: est. National Labor Board
		1934: est. National Labor Relations Board
		1935: National Labor Relations Act
117.	1933	Natural Resources Conservation Service

		1933: est. Soil Erosion Service 1994: renamed Natural Resources Conservation Service
118.	1933	Tennessee Valley Authority
119.	1934	Department of Housing and Urban Development (HUD) 1934: est. Federal Housing Administration 1937: est. U.S. Housing Authority 1938: est. Federal National Mortgage Association 1947: est. Housing and Home Finance Agency 1965: est. Department of Housing and Urban Development
120.	1934	National Archives and Records Administration
121.	1934	Export-Import Bank of the United States 1934: est. Export-Import Bank of Washington 1968: renamed Export-Import Bank of the United States
122.	1934	Federal Communications Commission (FCC)
123.	1934	Federal Deposit Insurance Corporation (FDIC)
124.	1934	Indian Arts and Crafts Board
125.	1934	National Archives and Records Administration (NARA) 1934: est. National Archives Establishment 1985: est. National Archives and Records Administration
126.	1934	National Mediation Board
127.	1934	Securities and Exchange Commission (SEC)
128.	1935	Office of the Federal Register
129.	1935	Railroad Retirement Board (RRB)
130.	1935	Rural Utilities Service 1935: est. Rural Electrification Administration

<table>
<tr><td></td><td></td><td>1994: reorganized into Rural Utilities Service</td></tr>
<tr><td>131.</td><td>1935</td><td>Social Security Administration (SSA)
1935: est. Social Security Board
1946: renamed Social Security Administration</td></tr>
<tr><td>132.</td><td>1936</td><td>U.S. Maritime Administration
1936: est. U.S. Maritime Commission
1950: est. U.S. Maritime Administration</td></tr>
<tr><td>133.</td><td>1937</td><td>Bonneville Power Administration</td></tr>
<tr><td>134.</td><td>1937</td><td>Office of Public and Indian Housing</td></tr>
<tr><td>135.</td><td>1938</td><td>Federal National Mortgage Association (Fannie Mae)</td></tr>
<tr><td>136.</td><td>1938</td><td>Risk Management Agency (Agriculture Department)
1938: est. Federal Crop Insurance Corporation
1996: est. Risk Management Agency</td></tr>
<tr><td>137.</td><td>1938</td><td>U.S. AbilityOne Commission
1938: est. Committee on Purchases of Blind Made Products
1971: est. The Committee for Purchase From People Who are Blind or Severely Disabled
2006: renamed AbilityOne</td></tr>
<tr><td>138.</td><td>1938</td><td>U.S. National Central Bureau - Interpol (Justice Department)</td></tr>
<tr><td>139.</td><td>1939</td><td>Administrative Office of the U.S. Courts</td></tr>
<tr><td>140.</td><td>1939</td><td>Defense Contract Audit Agency (DCAA)
1939: est. joint U.S. Navy and U.S. Army Air Corps audits
1942: est. joint audit coordination committees
(Navy, Army Air Corp, Ordnance Department)
1965: est. Defense Contract Audit Agency</td></tr>
<tr><td>141.</td><td>1939</td><td>National Geospatial-Intelligence Agency</td></tr>
</table>

1939: Engineer Reproduction Plant
assumes War Department Map
Collection
1942: est. Army Map Service
1968: renamed U.S. Army
Topographic Command
1972: renamed Defense Mapping
Agency Topographic Service
1996: est. National Imagery and
Mapping Agency
2003: renamed National Geospatial-
Intelligence Agency

142.   1939   Office of Environmental Management
1939: est. Manhattan Project
1947: est. Atomic Energy Commission
1975: est. Nuclear Regulatory
Commission
1975: est. Energy Research and
Development Administration
1977: est. Department of Energy
1989: est. Office of Environmental
Management

143.   1940   Bureau of the Fiscal Service
1940: est. Bureau of Public Debt (BPD)
1974: est. Financial Management
Service (FMS)
1984: FMS renamed Bureau of
Government Financial Operations
2012: est. Bureau of Fiscal Service
created from BPD & FMS

144.   1942   Central Intelligence Agency (CIA)
1942: est. Office of Strategic Services
1947: est. Central Intelligence Agency

145.   1942   Department of Energy (DOE)
1942: Manhattan Project
1946: Atomic Energy Commission
1977: Department of Energy

146.   1942   Voice of America
147.   1943   Joint Forces Staff College

1943: est. Army and Navy Staff College
1946: est. Armed Forces Staff College
2000: renamed Joint Forces Staff College

148. 1943 National War College
1943: est. Army-Navy Staff College
1946: est. National War College

149. 1943 Oak Ridge National Laboratory
1942: est. Oak Ridge
1943: est. Clinton Laboratories, currently named Oak Ridge National Laboratory

150. 1944 Southwestern Power Administration

151. 1945 Defense Technical Information Center
1945: est. Air Documents Research Center
1948: reorganized Central Air Documents Office
1951: renamed Armed Services Technical Information Agency
1963: renamed Defense Documentation Center
1979: renamed Defense Technical Information Center

152. 1945 U.S. Mission to the United Nations
1919: League of Nations
1945: United Nations

153. 1946 Centers for Disease Control and Prevention (CDC)

154. 1946 Council of Economic Advisers

155. 1946 Defense Intelligence Agency (DIA)
1946: est. U.S. Director of Central Intelligence
2005: est. Director of National Intelligence

156. 1946 Fulbright Foreign Scholarship Board

157. 1946 National Institute of Mental Health (NIMH)
1946: enacted National Mental Health Act

		1949: est. National Institute of Mental Health
158.	1946	Office of Refugee Resettlement
		1946: est. Corporate Affidavit Program
		1962: passed Migration and Refugee Assistance Act
		1982: est. Office of Refugee Resettlement
159.	1946	U.S. Air Force Reserve Command
		1946: est. Army Air Force Air Reserve
		1947: est. Continental Air Command
		1968: est. U.S. Air Force Reserve
		1997: renamed U.S. Air Force Reserve Command
160.	1946	U.S. Strategic Command
		1946: est. Strategic Air Command
		1992: est. Strategic Command
161.	1947	Bureau of International Labor Affairs
162.	1947	Defense Threat Reduction Agency (DTRA)
		1947: est. Defense Atomic Support Agency (DASA)
		1971: est. Defense Nuclear Agency (DNA)
		1996: est. Defense Special Weapons Agency (DSWA)
		1998: est. Defense Threat Reduction Agency by merger of DASA, DNA and DSWA
163.	1947	Federal Mediation and Conciliation Service
164.	1947	National Security Council
165.	1947	U.S. Air Force
166.	1948	Foreign Claims Settlement Commission
		1948: est. War Claims Commission
		1954: est. Foreign Claims Settlement Commission
167.	1949	General Services Administration
168.	1949	Radio Free Europe/Radio Liberty (RFE/RL)
		1949: est. RFE, 1951: est. Radio Liberation

		1959: renamed Radio Liberty
169.	1950	Court of Appeals for the Armed Forces
		1950: Court of Military Appeals
		1968: renamed United States Court of Military Appeals
170.	1950	National Science Foundation
171.	1950	Southeastern Power Administration
172.	1952	U.S. European Command
173.	1953	Agricultural Research Service
		1839: est. Library of the U.S. Department of Agriculture
		1862: est. U.S. Department of Agriculture
		1862: Morrill Land-Grant College Act
		1868: est. Division of Botany
		1877: est. U.S. Entomological Commission
		1884: est. Bureau of Animal Industry
		1887: Hatch Experiment Station Act
		1898: Congress authorizes testing of seeds
		1901: est. Bureau of Plant Industry
		1938: Agricultural Adjustment Act
		1953: est. Agricultural Research Service
174.	1953	Small Business Administration (SBA)
175.	1954	Saint Lawrence Seaway Development Corporation
176.	1955	Indian Health Service
177.	1955	President's Council on Physical Fitness, Sports and Nutrition
		1955: est. President's Council on Youth Fitness
		1963: renamed President's Council on Physical Fitness
		2010: renamed President's Council on Fitness, Sports and Nutrition
178.	1956	TRICARE Management
		1956: Dependents Medical Care Act
		1966: Military Medical Benefits

		Amendments
		1966: est. CHAMPUS
		1994: DoD Appropriation Act, 1997: est. Tricare
179.	1957	Citizens' Stamp Advisory Committee
180.	1957	Commission on Civil Rights
181.	1958	Defense Advanced Research Projects Agency (DARPA)
182.	1958	Federal Aviation Administration (FAA)
		1958: est. Federal Aviation Agency
		1966 renamed Federal Aviation Administration
183.	1958	John F. Kennedy Center for the Performing Arts
		1958: est. National Cultural Center
		1963: renamed John F. Kennedy Center for the Performing Arts
184.	1958	National Aeronautics and Space Administration (NASA)
185.	1960	Appalachian Regional Commission
186.	1960	Defense Information Systems Agency (DISA)
		1960: est. Defense Communications Agency
		1991: renamed Defense Information Systems Agency
187.	1961	Agency for International Development (USAID)
188.	1961	Delaware River Basin Commission
189.	1961	Defense Security Cooperation Agency (DSCA)
		1961: est. Defense Security Assistance Agency
		1998: renamed Defense Security Cooperation Agency
190.	1961	Economic Adjustment Office
191.	1961	Federal Executive Boards
192.	1961	National Agricultural Statistics Service
		For information prior to 1961, please reference The Story of U.S. Agricultural Estimates (Appendix B)

193.	1961	National Reconnaissance Office
194.	1961	Peace Corps
195.	1961	Office of Scientific and Technical Information

        1961: est. Office of Science and Technology
        1976: est. Office of Science and Technology Policy

196.	1961	U.S. Agency for International Development (USAID)
197.	1961	U.S. Trade and Development Agency
198.	1962	National Intelligence University
199.	1962	Office of Refugee Resettlement

        1962: Migration and Refugee Assistance Act
        1980: est. Office of Refugee Resettlement

200.	1962	U.S. Trade Representative
201.	1964	Administrative Conference of the United States
202.	1964	Federal Transit Administration

        1964: est. Urban Mass Transportation Administration
        1991: renamed Federal Transit Administration

203.	1964	Legal Services Corporation

        1964: Economic Opportunity Act
        1974: est. Legal Services Corporation

204.	1964	White House Commission on Presidential Scholars
205.	1965	Administration on Aging (AoA)
206.	1965	Centers for Medicare & Medicaid Services (CMS)
207.	1965	Economic Development Administration (EDA)
208.	1965	English Language Acquisition Office
209.	1965	Equal Employment Opportunity Commission (EEOC)
210.	1965	Federal Library and Information Center Committee

		1965: est. Federal Library Committee Currently: Federal Library and Information Center Committee
211.	1965	Housing Office (HUD)
212.	1965	National Endowment for the Arts
213.	1965	National Interagency Fire Center
		1965: est. Boise Interagency Fire Center 1933: renamed National Interagency Fire Center
214.	1966	Advisory Council on Historic Preservation
215.	1966	Department of Transportation (DOT)
216.	1966	Federal Railroad Administration
217.	1966	National Highway Traffic Safety Administration
		1966: est. U.S. Department of Transportation 1970: est. National Highway and Traffic Safety Administration
218.	1966	Overseas Private Investment Corporation
		1966: est. Private Investment Advisory Council 1969: est. Overseas Private Investment Council
219.	1967	Federal Judicial Center
220.	1967	National Park Foundation
221.	1968	U.S. Air Force Reserve Command
222.	1968	Fair Housing and Equal Opportunity (FHEO)
223.	1968	Government National Mortgage Association
224.	1968	Judicial Panel on Multidistrict Litigation
225.	1968	National Flood Insurance Program (NFIP)
226.	1968	National Institute of Justice
		1968: est. National Institute of Law Enforcement and Criminal Justice 1978: renamed National Institute of Justice
227.	1968	U.S. Access Board
		1968: Architectural Barriers Act 1973: est. Architectural and

		Transportation Barriers Compliance Board
		Currently: U.S. Access Board
228.	1968	Woodrow Wilson International Center for Scholars
229.	1969	Council on Environmental Quality
230.	1969	Inter-American Foundation
231.	1969	Minority Business Development Agency
		1969: est. Office of Minority Business Enterprise
		1979: renamed Minority Business Development Agency
232.	1970	Employee Benefits Security Administration (EBSA)
233.	1970	Environmental Protection Agency (EPA)
234.	1970	Federal Home Loan Mortgage Corporation (Freddie Mac)
235.	1970	Federal Law Enforcement Training Center
		1970: est. Consolidated Federal Law Enforcement Training Center
		1975: renamed Federal Law Enforcement Training Center
236.	1970	National Credit Union Administration
237.	1970	National Institute of Occupational Safety and Health
238.	1970	National Oceanic and Atmospheric Administration (NOAA)
239.	1970	National Ocean Service
240.	1970	Occupational Safety and Health Administration (OSHA)
241.	1970	Occupational Safety and Health Review Commission
242.	1970	Postal Regulatory Commission
		1970: est. Postal Rate Commission
		2006: renamed Postal Regulatory Commission
243.	1970	Susquehanna River Basin Commission
244.	1971	Amtrak, National Railroad Passenger Corporation

245.	1972	Animal and Plant Health Inspection Service
246.	1972	Bureau of Economic Analysis (BEA)
247.	1972	Consumer Product Safety Commission (CPSC)
248.	1972	Committee for the Implementation of Textile Agreements
249.	1972	Defense Security Service (DSS)

> 1972: est. Defense Investigative Service
> 1999: renamed Defense Security Service

250.	1972	Marine Mammal Commission
251.	1972	Uniformed Services University of the Health Sciences
252.	1973	Drug Enforcement Administration
253.	1973	Endangered Species Program
254.	1973	Federal Emergency Management Agency (FEMA)

> 1973: est. Federal Disaster Assistance Administration
> 1978: est. Federal Emergency Management Agency

255.	1973	Federal Financing Bank
256.	1973	Health Resources and Services Administration

> 1973: est. Health Resources Administration (HRA)
> 1973: est. Health Services Administration (HSA)
> 1982: est. Health Resources and Services Administration via merger of HRA and HSA

257.	1973	Inspectors General
258.	1973	Policy Development and Research (HUD)
259.	1973	Rehabilitation Services Administration (Education Department)
260.	1974	Administration for Native Americans
261.	1974	Chief Acquisition Officers Council
262.	1974	Congressional Budget Office (CBO)

263.	1974	Coordinating Council on Juvenile Justice and Delinquency Prevention
264.	1974	Federal Laboratory Consortium for Technology Transfer
		1974: organized
		1986: formally chartered
265.	1974	Joint Board for the Enrollment of Actuaries
266.	1974	Office of Juvenile Justice and Delinquency Prevention
267.	1974	Pension Benefit Guaranty Corporation (PBGC)
268.	1975	Arthritis and Musculoskeletal Interagency Coordinating Committee
269.	1975	Committee on Foreign Investment in the United States
270.	1975	Federal Election Commission
271.	1975	Harry S. Truman Scholarship Foundation
272.	1975	Japan-United States Friendship Commission
273.	1975	Nuclear Regulatory Commission
274.	1976	Commission on Security and Cooperation in Europe (Helsinki Commission)
275.	1976	Helsinki Commission
276.	1976	National Defense University
277.	1976	Office of Science and Technology Policy
278.	1977	Energy Information Administration
279.	1977	Federal Mine Safety and Health Review Commission
280.	1977	Mine Safety and Health Administration
281.	1977	National Bipartisan Commission on the Future of Medicare, 1977-1999
282.	1977	Surface Mining, Reclamation and Enforcement
283.	1977	U.S. Central Command (CENTCOM)
		1977: Presidential Directive 18
		1979: est. Rapid Deployment Force
		1980: est. Rapid Deployment Joint Task Force
		1983: est. U.S. Central Command
284.	1977	Western Area Power Administration

285.	1977	Washington Headquarters Services
286.	1977	White House Office of Administration
287.	1978	Bankruptcy Courts
288.	1978	Federal Labor Relations Authority
289.	1978	National Telecommunications and Information Administration
290.	1978	Office of Government Ethics
291.	1979	Bureau of Justice Statistics
292.	1979	Department of Education (ED)
293.	1979	Federal Financial Institutions Examination Council
294.	1979	Merit Systems Protection Board
295.	1979	U.S. Office of Special Counsel
296.	1979	U.S. Transportation Command
		1979: est. Joint Deployment Agency
		1987: est. Unified Transportation Command
297.	1980	African Development Foundation
298.	1980	Federal Student Aid Information Center
299.	1980	Holocaust Memorial Museum
300.	1980	International Trade Administration (ITA)
301.	1980	Military Postal Service Agency
302.	1980	Northwest Power and Conservation Council
303.	1981	Joint Military Intelligence College
		1962: est. Defense Intelligence School
		1993: renamed Joint Military Intelligence College
304.	1981	Veterans Employment and Training Service (VETS)
305.	1982	Bureau of Ocean Energy Management
		1982: est. Minerals Management Service
		2011: est. Bureau of Ocean Energy Management split from the Minerals Management Service
306.	1982	Department of Defense Inspector General
307.	1982	Federal Interagency Council on Statistical Policy
308.	1983	Information Resource Management College

309.	1983	Missile Defense Agency (MDA)
		1983: Strategic Defense Initiative
		1993: renamed Ballistic Defense Organization
		2002: renamed Missile Defense Agency
310.	1983	National Defense University iCollege
311.	1984	Arctic Research Commission
312.	1984	Institute of Peace
313.	1984	National Council on Disability (NCD)
314.	1984	State Justice Institute
315.	1984	U.S. Arctic Research Commission
316.	1984	U.S. Sentencing Commission
317.	1985	Agency for Toxic Substances and Disease Registry
318.	1985	Domestic Policy Council
319.	1986	Barry M. Goldwater Scholarship and Excellence in Education Program
320.	1986	Federal Retirement Thrift Investment Board
321.	1986	Federal Voting Assistance Program
		1986: Uniformed and Overseas Citizens Absentee Voting Act
		1993: National Voter Registration Act
		2002: Help America Vote Act,
322.	1986	James Madison Memorial Fellowship Foundation
323.	1987	Farm Credit System Insurance Corporation
324.	1987	Federal Consulting Group
325.	1987	Interagency Council on Homelessness
326.	1987	Nuclear Waste Technical Review Board
327.	1987	U.S. Special Forces Operations Command
328.	1988	Court of Appeals for Veterans Claims
329.	1988	Defense Nuclear Facilities Safety Board
330.	1988	National Constitution Center
331.	1988	National Indian Gaming Commission
332.	1988	National Technical Information Service
333.	1988	Office of National Drug Control Policy (ONDCP)
		1988: Anti-Drug Abuse Act

		1989: est. Office of National Drug Control Policy
334.	1988	Stennis Center for Public Service
335.	1988	U.S. Court of Appeals for Veterans Claims
336.	1990	Chemical Safety and Hazard Investigation Board
337.	1990	Chief Financial Officers Council
338.	1990	Defense Contract Management Agency
		1990: est. Defense Logistics Agency
		2000: renamed Defense Contract Management Agency
339.	1990	Federal Accounting Standards Advisory Board
340.	1990	Federal Geographic Data Committee
341.	1991	Defense Acquisition University
342.	1991	Defense Finance and Accounting Services (DFAS)
343.	1992	Bureau of Transportation Statistics
344.	1992	Inspector General of the House
345.	1992	Morris K. Udall and Stewart L. Udall Foundation
346.	1993	Computer Emergency Readiness Team (US CERT)
347.	1993	Corporation for National and Community Service
348.	1993	Defense Prisoner of War/Missing Personnel Office
349.	1993	National Drug Intelligence Center
350.	1993	National Economic Council
351.	1994	AmeriCorps
352.	1994	Community Oriented Policing Services (COPS)
353.	1994	National Institute of Food and Agriculture
		1994: est. Cooperative State research, Education, and Extension Service
		2008: est. National Institute of Food and Agriculture
354.	1994	Social Security Advisory Board
355.	1995	Office of Compliance

356.	1996	Education Resources Information Center (ERIC)
		1966: est. ERIC Collection
		2004:?: est. Education Resources Information Center
357.	1996	Interagency Alternative Dispute Resolution Working Group
358.	1996	Institute of Museum and Library Services
359.	1996	Presidio Trust
360.	1996	Radio Free Asia (RFA)
361.	1996	Surface Transportation Board
362.	1996	Taxpayer Advocacy Panel
363.	1997	Court Services and Offender Supervision Agency for the District of Columbia
364.	1997	Medicare Payment Advisory Commission
365.	1998	Commission on International Religious Freedom
366.	1998	Job Corps
367.	1998	Joint Fire Science Program
368.	1998	U.S. Commission on International Religious Freedom
369.	1999	Agency for Healthcare Research and Quality (AHRQ)
370.	1999	Broadcasting Board of Governors
371.	1999	Federal Interagency Committee for the Management of Noxious and Exotic Weeds
372.	1999	National Nuclear Security Administration
373.	1999	Open World Leadership Center
374.	1999	Public Diplomacy and Public Affairs (State Department)

2000s

375.	2000	Administration on Developmental Disabilities
376.	2000	U.S. Capitol Visitor Center
		2000: Groundbreaking
		2008: Officially open to the public
377.	2000	Federal Motor Carrier Safety Administration (FMCSA)
378.	2000	Vietnam Education Foundation
379.	2001	Bureau of Industry and Security
380.	2001	Bureau of Industry and Security
381.	2001	Office of Disability Employment Policy
382.	2001	Transportation Security Administration (TSA)
383.	2002	Chief Information Officers Council
384.	2002	Chief Human Capital Officers Council
385.	2002	Department of Homeland Security (DHS)
386.	2002	Institute of Education Sciences
387.	2002	U.S. Election Assistance Commission
388.	2002	U.S. Northern Command
389.	2004	Millennium Challenge Corporation
390.	2004	Office of Director of National Intelligence
391.	2004	Pipeline and Hazardous Materials Safety Administration
392.	2005	Research and Innovative Technology Administration
393.	2008	Federal Housing Finance Agency
394.	2009	Medicaid and CHIP Payment and Access Commission
395.	2009	Office of National AIDS Policy
396.	2010	Office of Servicemember Affairs
397.	2010	Fiscal Responsibility and Reform Commission
398.	2010	National Commission on Fiscal Responsibility and Reform
399.	2011	Bureau of Consumer Financial Protection
400.	2011	Consumer Financial Protection Bureau

And I stopped at 400. This list is not all inclusive nor is the list on USA.gov. For instance, I added the link to the U.S. National Arboretum. Nevertheless, the point has been made with the entries provided. Per our list we find that in the entire 17th and 18th Centuries the U.S. Federal Government created 30 agencies. In the 1800s a mere 44 agencies and in the 1900's a whopping 300 agencies. So far, in the first decade of the new millennium we have added 24 agencies compared to the 10 we started the 20th Century with putting us on track to crush that record. Yay!!! Well, yay if you're into the United States Federal Government being all things to all people.

DoT: Agencies. I won't debate the justification or contribution of any of these agencies, I'm sure they each have their merits. Rather, I list them for two reasons only: (1) to demonstrate Federal growth and (2) to demonstrate that after all of this there is still no effective alternative to chocolate. And, no, PGPR is not chocolate, it is not cocoa and it is not cocoa butter.

2000

	The Year 2000	What that looks like in 2013
Federal Corporate Income Tax	$235,654,894,000.00	$319,748,838,534.60
Federal Individual Income Tax	$1,137,077,702,000.00	$1,542,846,271,370.42
Federal Income	$2,096,916,925,000.00	$2,845,206,139,755.77
Federal Spending	$1,788,950,000,000.00	$2,427,340,569,877.88
Federal Surplus	+$236,241,000,000.00	$320,544,097,693.35
National Debt	$5,674,178,209,886.86	$7,699,020,637,566.98
Population	282,162,411	89.25%
Individual Income Tax Payers	127,590,000	In 2012: 89%
Percentage of Individual Income Tax Payers	45%	
Individual Income Tax Payer Burden	54%	
Individual Tax Burden	$7,431.60	$10,083.58
Individual Income Tax Payer Average	$8,911.97	$12,092.23
Individual National Debt Burden	$20,109.62	$27,285.78

IT'S NOT JUST INCOME TAX, YOU KNOW

"Excise taxes are taxes paid when purchases are made on a specific good, such as gasoline. Excise taxes are often included in the price of the product. There are also excise taxes on activities, such as on wagering or on highway usage by trucks. Excise Tax has several general excise tax programs. One of the major components of the excise program is motor fuel." Source: IRS, Excise Tax.

Basically, excise taxes are taxes that are often buried in the price and when that happens you don't even know you're paying them.

Below are a few excise taxes for your enjoyment. One not on the list started January 1, 2013 and it is a Medical Device excise tax of 2.3% so expect your hospital bill to be ever so slightly higher.

14	Aviation, gasoline
18	Domestic petroleum oil spill tax
19	ODC tax on imported products
20	Ozone-depleting chemicals (floor stock)
21	Imported petroleum products oil spill tax
22	Local telephone service & teletype/writer exchange service
26	Transportation of person by air
27	Use of international air travel facilities
28	Transportation of property by air
29	Transportation by water
30	Foreign Insurance Taxes, Life Insurance, sickness and accident policies, and annuity contracts
31	Obligations not Registered Form
33	Truck, trailer, and semitrailer chassis and bodies, and tractors
35	Kerosene: Tax on removal at terminal rack. Tax on taxable events other than removal at terminal rack
36	Coal-Underground mined-$ per ton
37	Coal-Underground mined-% of sales price

38	Coal-Surface mined-$ per ton
39	Coal-Surface mined-% of sales price
40	Gas guzzler tax
41	Sport fishing equipment (other than fishing rods and fishing poles)
42	Electric outboard motors
44	Bows, quivers, broadheads, and points
51	Alcohol and cellulosic biofuel sold but not used as fuel
60	Diesel Fuel: Tax on removal at terminal rack. Tax on taxable events other than removal at terminal rack. Tax on sale or removal of biodiesel mixture other than removal at terminal rack
62	Gasoline: Tax on removal at terminal rack Tax on taxable events other than removal at terminal rack. Tax on sale or removal of alcohol fuel mixture other than removal at terminal rack
64	Inland Waterways Fuel Use Tax
69	Kerosene for use in aviation
77	Kerosene for use in commercial aviation (other than foreign trade)
79	Other fuels
97	Vaccines
98	Ozone-Deplete chemicals (ODCs)
104	Diesel-water fuel emulsion
105	Dyed diesel fuel, LUST tax
106	Arrow shafts
107	Dyed kerosene, LUST tax
108	Taxable tires other than biasply or super single tires
109	Taxable biasply or super single tires (other than super single tires designed for steering)
110	Fishing rods and fishing poles
111	Kerosene for use in aviation, LUST tax on nontaxable uses, including foreign trade
112	Liquefied Petroleum Gas (LPG)
113	Taxable tires, super single tires designed for steering
114	Fishing tackle boxes
117	Biodiesel sold as but not used as fuel
118	P series fuels
119	LUST tax, other exempt removal

120   Compressed natural gas (CNG) (CGE = 126.67 cu. ft.)
121   Liquefied hydrogen
122   Any liquid fuel derived from coal (including peat)
       through the Fischer-Tropsch process
123   Liquid fuel derived from biomass
124   Liquefied natural gas (LNG)
125   LUST tax on inland waterways fuel use
140   Indoor Tanning

Of course, as mentioned in the section on Taxes, there are a few other types of tax besides Excise.

2012

	The Year 2012	What that looks like in 2013
Federal Corporate Income Tax	$281,461,580,000.00	$286,620,753,564.15
Federal Individual Income Tax	$1,331,160,000,000.00	$1,355,560,081,466.40
Federal Income	$2,150,891,380,000.00	$2,190,317,087,576.37
Federal Spending	$3,537,127,000,000.00	$3,601,962,321,792.26
Federal Deficit	$1,086,963,000,000.00	$1,106,886,965,376.78
National Debt	$16,066,241,407,385.00	$16,360,734,630,738.29
Population	313,873,685	100%
Individual Income Tax Payers	143,607,800	In 2012: 100%
Percentage of Individual Income Tax Payers	46%	
Individual Income Tax Payer Burden	62%	
Individual Tax Burden	$6,852.73	$6,978.34
Individual Income Tax Payer Average	$9,269.41	$9,439.32
Individual National Debt Burden	$51,186.97	$52,125.22

SOLUTIONS

DoT: Socrates. A Founding Father of Western Philosophy

DoT: Plato. A student of Socrates and a Founding Father of Western Philosophy and Science.

DoT: Aristotle. A student of Plato and, surprise, a Founding Father of Western Philosophy and Science.

When Philip II of Macedon was looking for a teacher for his thirteen year old son, Al, he wanted Aristotle. Yes, *that* Aristotle. Unfortunately, Aristotle was a bit reluctant and who can blame him what with Philip II of Macedon having spent a tremendous amount of time, money and energy burning Aristotle's hometown to the ground and killing or enslaving everybody he could get his hands on.

To continue, Philip II wanted Aristotle to teach his son so badly that he agreed to spend, again, a tremendous amount of time, money and energy putting everything back the way he found it. And who can blame *him*? He had a chance to get Aristotle and Aristotle was it. We're still talking about him today. So what did Aristotle teach young Al until he was seventeen?

Medicine, Morals, Religion, Philosophy, Logic and Art.

Today, some teachers will tell you that discussion, critical thinking and creative problem solving are taught in school.

Wrong.

Lets take Western Civilizations, for instance. I liked it. It was fun, it was interesting, my teacher was hot, it gave me a sense of the past. It was a lovely collection of facts.

Aristotle, had another perspective altogether.

Medicine: a way of thinking about the body;
Morals: a way of thinking about choices;
Religion: a way of thinking about our purpose in life;
Philosophy: a way of thinking about life;
Logic: a way of thinking critically;
Art: a way of seeing, a way of expressing, and a way of thinking creatively.

I guess two thousand three hundred and some odd years ago, more or less, they were more interested in writing history than reading about it. Alexander the Great certainly was.

Discussion, critical thinking and creative problem solving are byproducts of our educational process not courses specifically designed for and taught at critical times in our lives. Until that happens, and until those students grow up and start running the country - and voting for the people of their own ilk who will be running the country, you can forget solutions. So how do we get there?

I was channel surfing and a person was making a comment about children running along the lines of "just because they're smart doesn't mean they're disciplined." Analogously, just because we think doesn't mean we're thoughtful. Maybe we could have a high-school class of our own, not a seminar or a lecture or a one-off as the Brits say, but a genuine, dyed-in-the-wool, bred in the bone, class that ran for 3 or 4 years let's call it, oh, I don't know, how about Thinking and Conversing (because, you know, just because we talk doesn't mean we know how to have a conversation.) And in this class called Thinking and Conversing students could study Creative Problem Solving, Analysis, Logic, Morals, Ethics and Philosophy with the objective not to teach them what result to reach when they have a decision to make but rather how to use the tools in their heads so they can make that choice to the best possible effect. And the Conversing part could study the dynamics and practical use of Discussion, Compromise and Collaboration which in reality are tools you need for the Thinking part. We already know how to Debate and Argue.

81

ALTHOUGH

Although, it might not be bad to require our Congressmen to have term limits. Even then, of course, you could only hope. And I guess it would help if there were more Independents because they tend to act as a moderating influence. Of course, I'm not going to say throw them all out and hire (there's a funny word for people winning their office) no one but Independents. We only need about thirty percent.

THE DRAFT

Really, would it hurt if we got our members of the House and Senate in a manner similar to how we get members of a jury? Pick a random pool of candidates, vet them for mental and physical health and extenuating circumstances, post their profiles, viewpoints, and answers to publicly submitted questions onto the internet and then we vote. We could even push the envelope and say that those who are elected can run for reelection when their term expires in the same manner until their term limits are reached with the caveat that once they lose they are out and cannot run again. My feeling is that if Congress is filled with those people then Congress would not be raiding Social Security to fund deficits brought on by spending money we do not have in order to give individual Congressmen bragging rights, name recognition, and an unfair advantage in a race against nearly any contender. Of course, that's just my opinion. And I'm sure the billion dollars or so that is spent on national elections has nothing to do with it.

SPREADING THE LOAD

In 2012 the U.S. of A. had about 67 million tourists... France had 83 million but nothing beats a warm croissant. We also had about 10 million illegal immigrants. At any given time in 2012 the U.S population was 313 million plus 10 million + 184,000, which was the average number of tourists in the U.S. on any given day, so around 323 million people. All of whom were contributing taxes through purchases and only some of which were paying Income Tax. But this isn't about redistributing the burden of taxation because if they did that then the Federal Income Tax would likely go down and this book would be a bust. If it were, though, it would most likely be about hybrid taxation.

Hybrid taxation is nothing new. It's a combination of a Federal Income Tax and a Federal Sales Tax. It's been talked about but never agreed on in part because nobody has solid, reliable facts regarding how much would be raised. Or, if this were a collaborative body prone to thinking about things in a rational manner, they might decide to try a Hybrid Tax in one city, say Peoria, for a couple of years and compare the revenues generated. Then they might tweak it... I said tweak, not twerk, a little to tune it and try it in one State. Any tax system will work if you know where to set the rate. At this point, I would lobby that taxes of any kind, be they Federal, State or Local, on food, medicine and fuel should be removed.

DoT: Tweaking, as it is used here, and I'm quoting Google, is to make "a fine adjustment..." Granted, depending on who's doing the twerking we could be talking about fine adjustments, too... Yes, we certainly could. But I digress.

Twerking aside, I mean tweaking aside, you may recall that we spend a whopping amount of money trying to figure out how to pay a whopping amount of money. The likely result of a flat tax would be to reduce the former whopping amount of money quite a bit along with the size, influence and expenditures of the IRS. The supplemental sales tax would yield some help with the latter whopping amount of money from the 70 or 80 million extra people floating around the States every year.

SUMMARY

Lesser men might win or lose for personal or ideological differences while reasonable men might succeed or fail in the National Interest or, to put it another way, it is the difference between success and failure in the National Interest and winning or losing for personal or ideological gain. If thoughtful, reasonable men of good intention are unable to reach a consensus or a compromise then we are a mighty nation, indeed. When personal ambition becomes an obstacle to good intentions who should we blame?

By-the-way, Congress just passed its first trillion dollar budget! It brings a tear of joy my eyes to know that our representatives are working so hard that they're breaking records. By the way,

> this is $1
> this is $100
> this is $1,000
> this is $100,000
> this is $1,000,000
> this is $100,000,000
> this is $1,000,000,000

DoT: If somebody stacked a billion dollars then tipped it over so it formed one neat little line, and said you could only have what you could jog over and you were really greedy then you would have to jog for almost 68 miles to get all of it. Better yet, get in your car, find the straightest road you can and then drive for 67.9 miles.

> this is $100,000,000,000
> this is $1,000,000,000,000

but that's okay, it's not Congress' money.

It's your money.

And that's not even counting your State budget, City budget and Local budget. And I digress.

FINALLY

We are a Nation of over three hundred and twenty million people and our opinions are as broad as the horizons. One person may look at the growing pervasiveness of the United States Federal Government as a good thing given how small the world is and how wildly separated our society is from others. The taxes we pay and the way in which our money is spent are simply the cost of doing business. Another person may think of us all as birds in a gilded cage and all the while the predator stares in at us, saliva dripping from its lips and its voice purring ever so gently... I will protect you.

Somewhere in between is the likely truth. Our government is bursting with talented people who have dedicated their lives to making our lives better. There are also people, I like to hope who are only but a few, who taint this very same pool with far less than noble ambitions. And there are, of course, those who are along for the ride and doing as little as possible until they can retire. But this isn't really about any of those people, this is about Congress.

It is Congress that ultimately controls the size, strength and power of our Government. It is Congress that decides how much of our money to take and how much of our money to spend. And it is Congress whose responsibility it is to manage itself in the best interests of our Nation. And what is a Nation? The Federal Government? Hardly. A couple of beaches, a few trees and a mountain range? No, not that, either. A Nation is people.

Look around you, look across the street or in a mirror. You and nearly every person you see in these Fifty States are part of the same Nation. You are a member of the United States of America and until you start asking yourself what BETTER! means, and until you start insisting that your representatives ask the same questions, discuss from the same frames of reference and yes, even debate, with a level-headed, calm and rational demeanor and find creative solutions to complex problems, until you and every other member of our Nation changes, then Congress will not change... Of course, there's still that pesky inertia thing.

DoT: Inertia. "The vis insita, or innate force of matter, is a power of resisting by which every body, as much as in it lies, endeavours to preserve its present state, whether it be of rest or of moving uniformly forward in a straight line." Sir Isaac Newton.

In other words, a body at rest tends to stay at rest and a body in motion tends to stay in motion or a government that is growing is going to want to keep growing. Think about the U.S. Federal Government as a body moving not only through space but through time. It started small but as it moves through time it keeps growing. We tend to stand in one place, we live a few years and then it's over so we only see a snapshot but it's easy to extrapolate from the number of agencies where it is going. Because it's more efficient to do many things on a National level rather than a State or Local level more and more services will be provided by the Federal Government.

Another litmus test of the allocation of power in the United States is the accumulation of laws that either reduce liberties or increase and protect liberties. If one law a year is passed affirming individual liberties and three are passed reducing it (i.e. seat belts, smoking, warrantless searches) then in ten years there are thirty laws that take our liberties away and only ten that protect them.

We need thoughtful people in Congress who are mindful that not all growth is bad but that all growth should be keenly observed and the Balance of Power our own Founding Fathers as well as generations of men and women who were born here and immigrated here not only fought and died for but who also lived for is maintained. We can't all carry a gun and charge into battle but we can all know where we came from, respect the differences that make us the greatest Nation on Earth and shepherd the United States of America through our own time under the sun.

DoT: Finder's Fee. A Finder's Fee boils down to a reward for finding money. If the ideas presented here are actually used and save us even one percent that would represent an annual savings of ten billion dollars. Shouldn't this author then deserve a one-time finder's fee of 10% or a mere one billion dollars for putting all this together and ultimately being the impetus for reform...

No?...

Bummer.

APPENDIX A
TAXES THROUGH THE YEARS

This table is divided into 3 parts: the What, the How Much Was it Then, and the How Much Would That be in 2013 either as a dollar amount adjusted for inflation or as a percentage of whatever is current in order to get a sense of scale.

DoT: Table values. Nearly everything is estimated and, as far as was possible at the time of this writing, was based on July 1st of the year. For instance, the population changes throughout the year but on July 1st-ish it was about whatever.

Federal Corporate Income Tax
>This marks a trend in the proportions of Federal Income Tax paid by Corporations and the Federal Income Tax Payer.

Federal Individual Income Tax
>This is how much our Federal Government made strictly from Individual Federal Income Tax.

Federal Income
>This is all the money the U.S. Federal took in from taxes, fines, fees, whatever.

Federal Spending
>How much the Federal Government spent in that year and what that sum would have been in 2013, adjusted for inflation.

Federal Surplus or Deficit
>How much the Federal Government did not spend of the money they had or more often than not, how much they overspent.

National Debt
Add up all those Deficits that were never paid off and this is what you get, or as I like to put it, All Those Unpaid Bills. I was going to call this the 'Federal Debt' but 'National Debt' is more accurate.

Population
The population in the year and how that compares with the population in 2013.

Individual Income Tax Payers
The number of Individual Federal Income Tax payers.

In 1914 there were 357,958 taxpayers.

And the percentage of Individual Federal Income Tax Payers of 2012.

In 2012 there were 143,607,800.

357,958 is .2% of 143,607,800.

Percentage of Individual Income Tax Payers
The percentage of the Population who pay Federal Income Tax.

Income Tax Payer Burden
The percentage of the Total Federal Revenue that came from Individual Income Tax Payers:

Total Federal Individual Income Tax ÷ Total Federal Income

Individual Tax Burden
This would be the tax is it was evenly divided between every man, woman and child of the United States.

Individual Income Tax Payer Average
   The average Individual Federal Income Tax:

   Total Individual Income Tax ÷ Total Individual Income
   Tax Payers

Individual National Debt Burden
   We hire people to manage our Federal Money, we'll call
   them the Executive and Legislative branches of
   Government. They collect it, they invest it, they spend it
   but at the end of the day we're the ones who pick up the
   bill. The Individual National Debt Burden is the National
   Debt divided equally between every man, woman and child
   who is a U.S. Citizen so if you're part of a family of four you
   just go right ahead and multiply that number by four and
   that's what your family owes.

1913

	The Year 1913	What that looks like in 2013
Federal Corporate Income Tax	$0	$0
Federal Individual Income Tax	$0	$0
Federal Income	$344,424,453.85	$8,200,582,234.52
Federal Spending	$715,000,000.00	$17,023,809,523.81
Federal Deficit	Less Than $500,000.00	$11,904,761.90
National Debt	$2,916,204,913.66	$69,433,450,325.24
Population	97,225,000	30.75%
Federal Individual Income Tax Payers	0	0
Percentage of Individual Income Tax Payers	0%	
Income Tax Payer Burden	0%	
Individual Tax Burden	$3.54	$84.29
Individual Income Tax Payer Average	$0	$0
Individual National Debt Burden	$29.44	$700.95

1914

	The Year 1914	What that looks like in 2013
Federal Corporate Income Tax	$32,456,662.67	$754,806,108.60
Federal Individual Income Tax	$28,253,534.85	$657,058,950.00
Federal Income	$380,008,893.96	$8,837,416,138.60
Federal Spending	$726,000,000.00	$16,883,720,930.23
Federal Deficit	Less Than $500,000.00	$11,627,906.98
National Debt	$2,916,204,913.66	$67,818,718,922.33
Population	99,111,000	31.35%
Individual Income Tax Payers	357,598	In 2012: .2%
Percentage of Individual Income Tax Payers	.3%	
Individual Income Tax Payer Burden	7%	
Individual Tax Burden	$3.83	$89.07
Individual Income Tax Payer Average	$79	$1,837.21
Individual National Debt Burden	$29.42	$684.19

1930

	The Year 1930	What that looks like in 2013
Federal Corporate Income Tax	$275,588,648.53	$3,881,530,260.99
Federal Individual Income Tax	$247,502,042.64	$3,485,944,262.54
Federal Income	$580,615,592.31	$8,177,684,398.73
Federal Spending	$3,320,000,000.00	$46,760,563,380.28
Federal Surplus	+$738,000,000.00	$10,394,366,197.18
National Debt	$16,185,309,831.43	$227,962,110,301.83
Population	123,076,741	38.93%
Individual Income Tax Payers	1,872,268	In 2012: 1.3%
Percentage of Individual Income Tax Payers	1.5%	
Individual Income Tax Payer Burden	43%	
Individual Tax Burden	$4.72	$66.48
Individual Income Tax Payer Average	$132.19	$1,861.83
Individual National Debt Burden	$131.51	$1,852.25

1950

	The Year 1950	What that looks like in 2013
Federal Corporate Income Tax	$10,854,351,109.00	$105,382,049,601.94
Federal Individual Income Tax	$17,153,307,948.00	$166,536,970,368.93
Federal Income	$28,007,659,057.00	$271,919,019,970.87
Federal Spending	$42,562,000,000.00	$413,223,300,970.87
Federal Deficit	$3,100,000,000.00	$30,097,087,378.64
National Debt	$257,357,352,351.04	$2,498,615,071,369.32
Population	152,271,417	48.16%
Individual Income Tax Payers	51,841,335	In 2012: 36%
Percentage of Individual Income Tax Payers	34%	
Individual Income Tax Payer Burden	61%	
Individual Tax Burden	$183.93	$1,785.73
Individual Income Tax Payer Average	$330.88	$3,212.43
Individual National Debt Burden	$1,690.12	$16,408.93

1970

	The Year 1970	What that looks like in 2013
Federal Corporate Income Tax	$35,036,983,000.00	$211,066,162,650.60
Federal Individual Income Tax	$103,651,585,000.00	$624,407,138,554.22
Federal Income	$195,722,096,000.00	$1,179,048,771,084.34
Federal Spending	$195,649,000,000.00	$1,178,608,433,734.94
Federal Deficit	$2,800,000,000.00	$16,867,469,879.52
National Debt	$370,918,706,949.93	$2,234,450,041,867.05
Population	205,052,174	64.85%
Individual Income Tax Payers	78,370,000	In 2012: 55%
Percentage of Individual Income Tax Payers	38%	.
Individual Income Tax Payer Burden	53%	
Individual Tax Burden	$954.50	$5,750.00
Individual Income Tax Payer Average	$1,322.59	$7,967.41
Individual National Debt Burden	$1,808.90	$10,896.99

1980

	The Year 1980	What that looks like in 2013
Federal Corporate Income Tax	$72,379,610,000.00	$205,623,892,045.45
Federal Individual Income Tax	$287,547,782,000.00	$816,897,107,954.55
Federal Income	$519,375,273,000.00	$1,475,497,934,659.09
Federal Spending	$590,941,000,000.00	$1,678,809,659,090.91
Federal Deficit	$73,830,000,000.00	$209,744,318,181.82
National Debt	$907,701,000,000.00	$2,578,696,022,727.27
Population	227,224,681	71.87%
Individual Income Tax Payers	107,827,000	In 2012: 75%
Percentage of Individual Income Tax Payers	47%	
Individual Income Tax Payer Burden	55%	
Individual Tax Burden	$2,285.73	$6,493.55
Individual Income Tax Payer Average	$2,666.75	$7,575.99
Individual National Debt Burden	$3,994.73	$11,348.66

1990

	The Year 1990	What that looks like in 2013
Federal Corporate Income Tax	$93,133,625,000.00	$166,607,558,139.53
Federal Individual Income Tax	$463,441,656,000.00	$829,054,840,787.12
Federal Income	$959,114,855,000.00	$1,715,768,971,377.46
Federal Spending	$1,252,994,000,000.00	$2,241,491,949,910.55
Federal Deficit	$221,036,000,000.00	$395,413,237,924.87
National Debt	$3,233,313,451,777.25	$5,784,102,775,987.93
Population	249,464,396	78.91%
Individual Income Tax Payers	112,492,000	In 2012: 78%
Percentage of Individual Income Tax Payers	45%	
Individual Income Tax Payer Burden	48%	
Individual Tax Burden	$3,844.70	$6,877.82
Individual Income Tax Payer Average	$4,119.77	$7,369.89
Individual National Debt Burden	$12,961.02	$23,186.08

2000

	The Year 2000	What that looks like in 2013
Federal Corporate Income Tax	$235,654,894,000.00	$319,748,838,534.60
Federal Individual Income Tax	$1,137,077,702,000.00	$1,542,846,271,370.42
Federal Income	$2,096,916,925,000.00	$2,845,206,139,755.77
Federal Spending	$1,788,950,000,000.00	$2,427,340,569,877.88
Federal Surplus	+$236,241,000,000.00	$320,544,097,693.35
National Debt	$5,674,178,209,886.86	$7,699,020,637,566.98
Population	282,162,411	89.25%
Individual Income Tax Payers	127,590,000	In 2012: 89%
Percentage of Individual Income Tax Payers	45%	
Individual Income Tax Payer Burden	54%	
Individual Tax Burden	$7,431.60	$10,083.58
Individual Income Tax Payer Average	$8,911.97	$12,092.23
Individual National Debt Burden	$20,109.62	$27,285.78

2012

	The Year 2012	What that looks like in 2013
Federal Corporate Income Tax	$281,461,580,000.00	$286,620,753,564.15
Federal Individual Income Tax	$1,331,160,000,000.00	$1,355,560,081,466.40
Federal Income	$2,150,891,380,000.00	$2,190,317,087,576.37
Federal Spending	$3,537,127,000,000.00	$3,601,962,321,792.26
Federal Deficit	$1,086,963,000,000.00	$1,106,886,965,376.78
National Debt	$16,066,241,407,385.00	$16,360,734,630,738.29
Population	313,873,685	100%
Individual Income Tax Payers	143,607,800	In 2012: 100%
Percentage of Individual Income Tax Payers	46%	
Individual Income Tax Payer Burden	62%	
Individual Tax Burden	$6,852.73	$6,978.34
Individual Income Tax Payer Average	$9,269.41	$9,439.32
Individual National Debt Burden	$51,186.97	$52,125.22

APPENDIX B
REFERENCES

1. United States of America Government
   a. USA.gov
      i. www.usa.gov
      ii. the A-Z Index of Federal Departments and Agencies
         1. www.usa.gov/directory/federal/index.shtml
            ?utm_source=Links%2BPage&utm_mediu
            m=Static%2BPage&utm_campaign=New%2
            BLinks%20Page%20Usage
   b. Census Bureau
      i. www.census.gov
      ii. American Fact Finder
         1. http://factfinder2.census.gov/faces/nav/jsf
            /pages/index.xhtml
      iii. Federal, State, & Local Governments
         1. www.census.gov/govs
      iv. Government Employment & Payroll
         1. www.census.gov/govs/apes
         2. No. HS-46. Governmental Employment and
            Payrolls: 1946 to 2001
            a. www.census.gov/statab/hist/HS-
               46.pdf
      v. Historical National Population
         1. www.census.gov/population/estimates/nati
            on/popclockest.txt
      vi. U.S and World Population Clock
         1. www.census.gov/popclock
   c. Central Intelligence Agency
      i. www.cia.gov
      ii. The World FactBook
         1. www.cia.gov/library/publications/the-
            world-factbook/fields/2128.html

d. Congressional Budget Office
    i. www.cbo.gov
    ii. Federal Debt and the Statutory Limit, June 2013
        1. www.cbo.gov/publication/44324
e. Department of Labor
    i. www.dol.gov
    ii. Bureau of Labor Statistics
        1. www.bls.gov
        2. CPI Inflation Calculator
            a. www.bls.gov/data/inflation_calculat or.htm
f. Department of State
    i. http://fpc.state.gov/6172.htm
    ii. Foreign Policy Roles of the President and Congress
        1. June 1,1999, Richard Grimmett

g. Department of the Treasury
    i. www.treasury.gov
    ii. Bureau of Fiscal Service
        1. www.fiscal.treasury.gov
        2. TreasuryDirect
            a. www.treasurydirect.gov/tdhome.ht
                m
            b. Historical Debt Outstanding -
                Annual
                    i. www.treasurydirect.gov/govt
                        /reports/pd/histdebt/histde
                        bt.htm
    iii. Internal Revenue Agency
        1. A Brief History of the IRS
            a. www.irs.gov/uac/Brief-History-of-
                IRS
        2. Excise Tax
            a. www.irs.gov/Businesses/Small-
                Business-&-Self-Employed/Excise-
                Tax
        3. IRS Tax Type Numbers and Codes
            a. www.irs.gov/pub/irs-pdf/p4990.pdf
        4. The Complexity of the Tax Code
            a. www.irs.gov/pub/irs-
                utl/08_tas_arc_msp_1.pdf
        5. SOI Tax Stats Archive - 1863 to 1999 Annual
            Reports and IRS Data Books
            a. www.irs.gov/uac/SOI-Tax-Stats-
                Archive-1863-to-1999-Annual-
                Reports-and-IRS-Data-Books
        6. Taxpayer Advocate Service
            a. www.taxpayeradvocate.irs.gov

h.   Federal Aviation Administration
     i.   www.faa.gov
     ii.   A Brief History of the FAA
         1.   www.faa.gov/about/history/brief_history
i.   Library of Congress
     i.   www.loc.gov
     ii.   IRS History
         1.   www.loc.gov/rr/business/hottopic/irs_history.html
j.   National Archives
     i.   www.archives.gov
     ii.   Records of the National Security Agency
         1.   www.archives.gov/research/guide-fed-records/groups/457.html
     iii.   The Story of U.S. Agricultural Estimates
         1.   https://archive.org/details/storyofusagricul1088unit
     iv.   The United States Constitution
         1.   www.archives.gov/exhibits/charters/constitution.html
     v.   The Bill of Rights
         1.   www.archives.gov/exhibits/charters/bill_of_rights_transcript.html
     vi.   Constitution Amendments 11 - 27
         1.   www.archives.gov/exhibits/charters/constitution_amendments_11-27.html
k.   Office of the Historian
     i.   http://history.state.gov

l. Senate
    i. www.senate.gov
    ii. Congressional Salaries and Allowances
        1. http://www.senate.gov/CRSReports/crs-
            publish.cfm?pid='0E%2C*PL%5B%3D%23P
            %20%20%0A
    iii. Introduction to the Federal Budget Process
        1. www.senate.gov/CRSReports/crs-
            publish.cfm?pid=%26*2%3C4Q%3CS:%0A
m. White House
    i. www.whitehouse.gov
    ii. Historical Tables
        1. www.whitehouse.gov/omb/budget/Historic
            als
            a. Historical Tables Summary of
                Receipts, Outlays and Surpluses or
                Deficits (-) 1789-2018
    iii. Impacts and Costs of the Government Shutdown
        1. www.whitehouse.gov/blog/2013/11/07/imp
            acts-and-costs-government-shutdown

2. American Petroleum Institute
   a. www.api.org
   b. Motor Fuel Taxes
      i. www.api.org/oil-and-natural-gas-overview/industry-economics/fuel-taxes
3. Center on Budget and Policy Priorities
   a. www.cbpp.org
   b. A Guide to Statistics on Historical Trends in Income Inequality
      i. www.cbpp.org/cms/?fa=view&id=3629
4. Dave Manuel.com
   a. www.davemanuel.com
   b. The Inflation Calculator
      i. www.davemanuel.com/inflation-calculator.php
   c. US Government Spending
      i. www.davemanuel.com/us-government-spending.php
   d. A History of Debt in the United States
      i. www.davemanuel.com/history-of-debt-in-the-united-states.php
5. The Endowment for Human Development
   a. www.ehd.org
   b. Grasping Large Numbers
      i. www.ehd.org/science_technology_largenumbers.php
6. Monticello Museum
   a. www.Monticello.org
   b. Research and Collections
      i. Firearms
      ii. http://www.monticello.org/site/research-and-collections/firearms
7. Philosophiæ Naturalis Principia Mathematica by Sir Isaac Newton
8. Princeton University
   a. www.princeton.edu
   b. Testing Theories of American Politics: Elites, Interest Groups, and Average Citizens
      i. www.princeton.edu/~mgilens/Gilens%20homepage%20materials/Gilens%20and%20Page/Gilens%20and%20Page%202014-Testing%20Theories%203-7-14.pdf
9. Sales Tax Institute
   a. www.salestaxinstitute.com/resources/rates

10. Standard & Poor's
    a. www.standardandpoors.com
    b. Impact Of The Debt Ceiling Debate On The U.S. Economy
       - Getting Worse By The Day
       i. www.standardandpoors.com/ratings/articles/en/u
          s/?assetID=1245358642459
11. Tax Foundation.org
    a. http://taxfoundation.org
    b. U.S. Federal Individual Income Tax Rates History, 1913-
       2013
       i. http://taxfoundation.org/article/us-federal-
          individual-income-tax-rates-history-1913-2013-
          nominal-and-inflation-adjusted-brackets
    c. State Individual Income Tax Rates, As of January 1, 2013
       i. http://taxfoundation.org/article_ns/state-
          individual-income-tax-rates-2000-2013
12. The Telegraph
    a. www.telegraph.co.uk
    b. The US is an Oligarchy, Study Concludes by Zachary
       Davies Boren
       i. www.telegraph.co.uk/news/worldnews/northameri
          ca/usa/10769041/The-US-is-an-oligarchy-study-
          concludes.html
13. U.S. Government Revenue.com
    a. www.usgovernmentrevenue.com
    b. Revenue History
       i. www.usgovernmentrevenue.com/revenue_history
14. Wikipedia
    a. http://en.wikipedia.org
       i. Various Federal agencies
    b. Forms of Government
       i. http://en.wikipedia.org/wiki/Category:Forms_of_
          government

www.ingramcontent.com/pod-product-compliance
Lightning Source LLC
Chambersburg PA
CBHW070159290526
45789CB00002B/838